WENDY L. JONES

Talking on Paper: Alexander Pope's Letters

ELS Editions
Department of English
University of Victoria
Victoria, BC
Canada V8W 3W1
www.elseditions.com

Founding Editor: Samuel L. Macey

General Editor: Luke Carson

Printed by CreateSpace

English literary studies monograph series
ISSN 0829-7681 ; 50
ISBN-10 0-920604-52-8
ISBN-13 978-0-920604-52-6

CONTENTS

The majority of studies on Alexander Pope's letters spring from an emotional, not an analytical, response to the correspondence, whose publication, ironically, the poet believed would mean more to his reputation than all his other works together.[1] Critical evaluations of the letters tend to remain obstinately rooted in the moral indignation Pope's Victorian editors expressed on their discovery that he had not only surreptitiously engineered publication of his correspondence in his own lifetime but also had misdirected a number of letters and conflated or spliced or fabricated others.

The insidious nature of this phenomenon can be adduced from the fact that even recent studies of Pope's letters usually fail to distinguish, in their general pronouncements on his correspondence, between those letters revised by Pope for publication and those collected and published posthumously. George Sherburn's edition of the correspondence (1956), however, makes it clear that only about ten percent of the letters printed therein were 'doctored' by Pope.

That Pope intended a selected, carefully-edited portion of his letters to be published has not been seriously questioned since C.W. Dilke discovered the Caryll transcripts in 1864.[2] That he meant for these letters to be regarded as 'literature' is indicated by his inclusion, after 1737, of the authorized edition of his correspondence in his *Works* in prose. Oddly enough, the issue of Pope's choice of the 'familiar letter' as a literary genre in which to express himself has never been directly addressed, although it has been approached obliquely by those critics who discuss Pope's indebtedness to epistolary predecessors and precedents.

While such comparisons are illuminating and essential for a full appreciation of Pope's letters, they must be accompanied by a recognition that Pope was very much a letter writer of his own age. The same sensitivity to the subtle nuances of feeling, taste and opinion which contributed to make him the foremost poet of the early eighteenth century is no less significant in Pope's choice of the familiar letter as a vehicle of expression.

A chronological listing of the critical response to Pope's letters, from their first appearance in 1735 up to the present day, reveals a shift in assessments appearing after Pope's death; the eclipse of neoclassicism, with a consequent re-evaluation of epistolary standards, coincided with a renewed interest in whether Pope was involved in even the supposedly 'pirated,' 'unauthorized' 1735 edition. But the contemporary reading public to which Pope directed his epistolary efforts warmly applauded them. It was a public nurtured on the humanist tradition of the letter published as literature intended to instruct or to entertain; as this was the tradition to which Pope appealed in publishing his own correspondence, it is one with which we must become familiar before looking at the letters themselves. We can then place Pope's letters in the context of the Augustan literary scene, an exercise revealing him to have been very much a letter writer of his time, sharing his contemporaries' beliefs and expectations concerning epistolary literature. It is also instructive to relate Pope's editions of his letters to the onslaught of pamphlet attacks on his writings, character and person which constituted an integral feature of Pope's poetical career. Finally, it may be seen that Pope, in certain respects, transcended purely personal motives in publishing his letters to accomplish broader aims.[3]

CHAPTER ONE

Pope's Letters
The Critical Heritage

On 7 May 1735 Edmund Curll, notorious piratical Augustan bookseller, received fifty copies of *Letters of Mr. Pope, and Several Eminent Persons*.[1] These books had been delivered to Curll by a mysterious individual who identified himself only as 'P. T.' On 12 May he sent Curll one hundred and ninety more copies, although this 'afternoon edition' varied slightly from the first fifty copies delivered to Curll.[2] Curll immediately began printing his own edition of the letters, which he entitled *Mr. Pope's Literary Correspondence*. A number of London booksellers followed suit, with twenty separate editions claiming to represent either Pope's 'Literary Correspondence' or his 'Letters' appearing between 12 May and 21 December.[3]

There was suspicion from the very start that Pope had somehow been involved in the printing and publication of *Letters of Mr. Pope*. The circumstances of its publication are as follows. In 1733 Curll advertised for facts and documents for a life of Pope. On 11 October 'P. T.' responded by letter, sending Curll spurious but plausible information about Pope, and promising Curll more should he signal interest by placing a message to that effect in the *Daily Advertiser* for 18 October.[4] Curll failed to place the advertisement and was contacted by P. T. again in a letter dated 15 November 1733, offering him a 'large Collection of [Pope's] *Letters*, from the former Part of his Days to the Year 1727.'[5] Unable to arrange a meeting with P. T., Curll refused. Sixteen months later, however, Curll approached Pope directly, sending him P. T.'s letters and asking for Pope's compliance in his scheme of publishing the poet's biography. Pope rejected Curll's advances publicly by placing the following notice in the *Daily Post-Boy* of 3 April 1735:

Whereas *A. P.* hath received a Letter from *E. C.* Bookseller pretending that a Person, the initials of whose Name are *P. T.* hath offered the said *E. D.* to print a large collection of Mr. *P.*'s Letters, to which *E. C.* requires an Answer, *A. P.* having never had, nor intending to have, any private Correspondence with the said *E. C.* gives it him in this Manner. That he knows no such Person as *P. T.* that he believes he hath no such Collection, and that he thinks the whole a Forgery, and shall not trouble himself at all about it.[6]

P. T., claiming to have seen Pope's notice, wrote to Curll on 4 April. He told Curll he had already had the letters printed, and Curll negotiated for the copy. Curll never met P. T. but dealt with a man in a clergyman's gown calling himself R. Smythe. Curll received a total of 240 copies in two instalments but, shortly after the second delivery, Curll and the books were seized by officers of the House of Lords. An advertisement heralding the imminent publication of Pope's letters, including a list of correspondents, which Curll had been persuaded to place by Smythe in the *Daily Post-Boy* of 12 May had suggested that letters from peers would be included in the collection: the unauthorized printing of letters by lords then represented an illegal 'breach of privilege'.

In the event, the volumes were discovered to contain Pope's letters to peers but none from them; Curll was released and the books were returned to him. Pope now offered by advertisement a reward to twenty guineas for information about this publication of his letters and twice that sum for the identity of P. T. and the whereabouts of R. Smythe. Pope also advertised in the *London Gazette* of 15 July 1735 that he would republish so much of his correspondence as was genuine as well as a few additional letters. This 'official' or authorized edition of Pope's letters appeared in May 1737.

It was Curll who first raised the alarm, suspecting that Pope's involvement in the affair was deeper than the poet ever acknowledged. The apparently indignant Pope had published his own account of Curll's publication of his letters, entitled *A Narrative of the Method by Which the Private Letters of Mr. Pope had been Procur'd and publish'd by Edmund Curll, Bookseller*, on 12 June 1735. This *Narrative* may have inspired Curll's doubts on the grounds that Pope was too well-informed regarding the details of the transactions between the bookseller and P. T. and Smythe. A month later Curll included a rebuttal blaming Pope for the publication in his second volume of *Mr. Pope's Literary Correspondence.*[7] In addition to this rebuttal, entitled *The Initial Correspondence, or, Anecdotes of the Life and Family of Pope*, this second volume also contained a prefatory letter addressed to Pope which identifies P. T. as 'Trickster Pope' and describes Pope's letters as collected and published by Pope's own direction.[8]

While it was not likely that Curll, infamous for unscrupulously procuring and publishing anything that might turn a profit, was to be believed rather than Pope, a footnote to a libellous poem on Pope and Colley Cibber, *Sawney and Colley*, published in 1742, suggests that some were convinced by Curll's *Initial Correspondence*.[9] Of course, Pope's enemies were always prepared to believe the worst. In 1743 in *The Egotist* Cibber hinted that Pope had anonymously sold his letters and then, to be paid twice for the same copy, published a 'genuine' edition.[10] In 1754 Lady Mary Wortley Montagu also laid the charge of avarice at Pope's door; in a letter to Lady Bute of 23 June she claimed that:

> Pope courted with the utmost assiguity all the old men from whom he could hope a Legacy . . . There cannot be a stronger proofe of his being capable of any Action for the sake of Gain than publishing his Literary Correspondence, which lays open such a mixture of Dullness and iniquity that one would imagine it visible even to his most passionate admirers.[11]

There are the exceptions, however. In general, as Dr. Johnson observed, 'Pope's private correspondence . . . filled the nation with praises of his candour, tenderness, and benevolence, the purity of his purposes, and the fidelity of his friendship.'[12] William Broome, one of Pope's collaborators in the Homer translations and thus no blind enthusiast where the poet's virtues were concerned, voiced contemporary opinion in observing that the letters would undoubtedly benefit rather than harm Pope's reputation:

> With the good they certainly do you honour, and the worst that the ill-natured can say is what is no dishonour . . . the humane companion, the dutiful and affectionate son, the compassionate and obliging friend, appear so strongly almost in every page, that I assure you I had rather be the owner of the writer's heart than of the head that has honoured England with Homer, his Essays, Moral Epistles, &c.

Similarly, Swift, on receiving a copy of Pope's authorized quarto edition of letters, remarked in a letter to Pope of 1737 that:

> my opinion is, that there might be collected from them the best System that ever was wrote for the Conduct of human life, at least to shame all reasonable men out of their Follies and Vices.[13]

This common view of Pope's published letters as representing the elevating spectacle of the moral life of a poet and his illustrious friends prompted the philanthropist Ralph Allen to urge Pope in 1735 to publish an 'authentic' edition and to offer him generous financial assistance to this end. As Owen Ruffhead observed in his 1769 biography of Pope: 'no sooner had [Allen] read our author's letters, than he *loved* him for the goodness and virtues of his heart: and ever after entertained the most cordial affection for him.'[14]

Ironically, Ruffhead's own glowing praise of Pope's letters signalled the end of Pope's popularity both as letter writer and as poet: he had begun to be championed by the wrong people and for the wrong reasons. Ruffhead began his analysis by quite properly pointing out parallels between Pope's letters and those written by Voiture and Balzac, two popular seventeenth-century French letter writers who undoubtedly served as Pope's models. But Ruffhead spoilt his commendation of the poet's letters by praising them for the very qualities they patently lacked: simplicity and freshness.[15] Thomas Gray, more than twenty years earlier, in 1746, had provided one of the last balanced appraisals of Pope's letters:

> it is not from what he told me about himself that I thought well of [Pope], but from a Humanity & Goodness of Heart, ay, & Greatness of Mind, that runs thro his private Correspondence, not less apparent than are a thousand little Vanities & Weaknesses mixed with those good Qualities, for no body ever took him for a Philosopher.[16]

Gray's own letters, with William Cowper's and Horace Walpole's, superseded Pope's in popularity when, in the latter half of the eighteenth century, the standards used to judge a good letter changed: classical allusions and learned wit were succeeded by a preference for the epistolary ease and naturalness which Ruffhead, in his blundering panegyric, had attributed to Pope. Ironically, Gray's sensitive praise appeared in a letter to Walpole who, thirty years later, perhaps motivated in part by a spirit of professional rivalry, alleged that 'Mr. Pope laboured his letters as much as the *Essay on Man*, and as they were written to everybody, they do not look as if they had been written to anybody.'[17]

The damage to the reputation of Pope's letters inflicted by changing literary standards applied to epistolary writing was heightened by a revival of interest in the circumstances surrounding the 1735 'unauthorized' publication of his correspondence. This was especially true after Johnson's influential *Life of Pope* appeared in 1781. It is not that Johnson failed to provide intelligent or sympathetic analysis; rather, he also offered such a plausible account of his reasons for believing that Pope had surreptitiously engineered Curll's publication of his letters, that Pope's complicity came to be generally accepted. Johnson perceptively noted that 'Pope may be said to write always with his reputation in his head.'[18] This insight, however, only contributed to the severity of his opinion of this particular publication:

> If the Letters of Pope are considered merely as compositions they seem to be premeditated and artificial. It is one thing to write because there is something which the mind wishes to discharge, and another to solicit the imagination because ceremony or vanity requires something to be written.[19]

The Reverend William Bowles, Pope's next editor, crossed swords with a number of individuals over his unsympathetic portrayal of Pope. Bowles and the Reverend Whitwell Elwin, who followed Bowles in denouncing Pope's morals as revealed in his letters, provoked Byron's famous cry, 'We must rescue Pope from the priests!'[20] The section of Pope's correspondence entitled 'Letters to Ladies', written in a style directly derived from Voiture, proved particularly offensive to Bowles, who found them 'constrained, affected, full of false wit, and false gaiety.'[21] Pope's occasional lapse into coarseness also upset him, but Byron concluded that the licentiousness which Bowles perceived in his letters was 'less the tone of Pope than the tone of the time.'[22]

C. W. Dilke's chance discovery of the Caryll transcripts effectively put an end to a century's speculation although, surprisingly, at least one of Pope's subsequent editors chose to discount the unambiguous evidence of Pope's complicity in the Curll publication which the transcripts represented.[23] The transcripts, consisting of contemporary copies of the original letters Pope had sent his old friend John Caryll, made it apparent that Pope had 'remodelled some parts of his correspondence before publication, correcting, re-writing, conflating two or three letters into one, re-addressing letters to different persons, and so on.'[24] As these modifications appeared not only in Pope's 'authorized' 1737 edition but also in Curll's supposedly pirated 1735 edition, it became plain that Pope had, after all, been responsible for even the earlier edition.

In general, Pope's Victorian editors placed the worst possible construction on Pope's motives in thus 'cooking' his correspondence. For example, on discovering that Pope had re-addressed letters originally sent to Caryll to Addison and William Wycherley, whose names had long been linked with Pope's in scandal, the Victorians assumed that Pope self-servingly had wanted to emphasize his intimacy with these great writers and to 'put his own conduct towards them "in a good light".'[25]

Of all Pope's Victorian editors, Elwin was the most indignant. In 1871, in the first volume of his edition of Pope's *Works*, he asserted that the chief importance of the letters lay in their 'relation to the morality of Pope,' and that 'we have to decide whether his letters are not many of them fraudulent, and the circumstances attending their publication a series of ignominious plots, infamous false accusations, and impudent lies.'[26]

Few, however, were willing to go quite as far in condemning Pope as Elwin, and in 1872, when the first two volumes of Pope's poetry and the first three of his letters had appeared, the outcry against Elwin's harsh treatment of his subject was such that Elwin resigned his editorship, and W. J. Courthope undertook the completion of the work.[27] Adolphus Ward's 1869 Globe edition of Pope's *Poetical Works* had been somewhat more sympathetic. While Ward deplored the effects of Pope's editing of his letters, whereby he 'succeeded in depriving [them] of every vestige of natural freshness,' Ward generously championed Pope who, he believed, had served literature ardently all his life for neither fame, place, pay nor power but 'for her own sake.'[28]

The accusations return in Leslie Stephen's 1880 *Alexander Pope* in which Stephen likened Pope to Blifil in his dealings with Squire Allworthy's prototype, Ralph Allen. While Stephen thought 'there is scarcely a more interesting volume in the language than that which contains the correspondence of Swift, Bolingbroke, and Pope,' he was less taken with the rest of the letters, which he judged by the epistolary standards which had come to the fore shortly after Pope's death:

> We should be, indeed, disappointed were we to expect in Pope's letters what we find in the best specimens of the art: the charm which belongs to a simple outpouring of friendly feeling in private intercourse; the sweet playfulness of Cowper, or the grave humour of Gray, or even the sparkle and brilliance of Walpole's admirable letters.[29]

The tide of critical opinion began to turn in Pope's favour in 1930 when Edith Sitwell argued that Pope's 'uncandid' behaviour in secretly revising his letters and surreptitiously publishing them derived from his 'longing to be regarded not only as a great poet, but as a great and good man.'[30] In 1934 George Sherburn, in his biographical study, *The Early Career of Alexander Pope*, pertinently observed that 'most letters printed in the eighteenth century were revised for publication'; second, that 'it is doubtful if Pope has so falsified his letters as to change the story fundamentally'; and, third, that usually Pope's revisions of his letters 'had no other purpose than literary effect.'[31] Similarly, Norman Ault (1949) contended that Pope 'thought of his letters as the raw material of literature rather than the finished product'; the problem thus presented by the letters returned to Pope upon correspondents' deaths or upon his recalling them was one of editorial method.[32]

Sherburn's publication of the *Correspondence* in 1956 heralded a new era in literary scholarship dealing with Pope's letters. Of the more than two thousand letters included in this edition, less than three hundred had been printed by Pope, and of these, Sherburn reproduced nearly one third from reliable transcripts or from autograph copies. As Sherburn pointed out, Pope himself 'published only a very small part of his correspondence,' and thus most of Pope's surviving letters escaped his revision.[33] Sherburn's edition was unique in a number of ways. It helpfully identified the various editions or manuscript copies from which the letters it printed were taken; it placed in brackets passages of letters omitted by Pope or by subsequent editors of the correspondence; and it observed a chronological arrangement.

Sherburn's edition offered literary critics an unprecedented opportunity to take an overall view of Pope's letters: a view undistorted either by Pope's or by subsequent editor's revisions. Maynard Mack, for example, was moved to commend it for a presentation of Pope as letter writer 'hewn free of Victorian prejudice and misinformation.'[34] He concluded that, contrary to popular belief, Pope's revisions lay 'mainly in the direction of elevation and generalization.'[35] John Butt similarly inferred from Sherburn's edition that none of Pope's editorial changes had been major ones, that in comparing the letters Pope printed with the originals or with independent transcripts, we see that what he omitted were 'trivialities and occasional profanities, but that his principal revisions were purely stylistic.'[36] The conclusion Butt reached was that the letters Pope published were designed to exhibit 'the man of plain living, high thinking and unimpeachable integrity,' but that this was the view of himself Pope 'discovered in his letters as he reread them, rather than the view that he designedly wrote into them.'[37]

One might have expected that Sherburn's edition would have exorcised, once and for all, the spectre which has haunted Pope's reputation since the 1735 publication: a spectre compounded of the suspicions that Pope had deliberately misrepresented himself and his friends in revising his correspondence and that he was guilty of avarice, vindictiveness and vanity in publishing it. Such was not the case. The Victorians' harsh judgments continue to color critical response to Pope's letters up to the present day. Indicative of this phenomenon is a review of a recent book on Pope's letters which concludes that 'in the end, for all [the author's] individual insights, his book also leaves the impression that it is less an introduction to Pope's letters than an *apologia* for Pope himself.'[38]

CHAPTER TWO

The Contemporary Context

It has often been observed that the golden days when Swift, Prior, Pope and Gay were the intimates of Lord Treasurer Oxford and of Secretary of State Bolingbroke represented the closest English parallel to the Augustan Age of Rome, when Augustus and Maecenas had similarly favored the best writers of their age — Virgil, Horace and Livy — with their patronage and friendship. It was a parallel cherished by Dryden and Goldsmith who, among others, dubbed the reign of Queen Anne an 'Augustan' age of England. The parallel did not confine itself to focusing on the alliance between the literary and the political; it naturally extended to a number of other comparisons between early eighteenth-century England and the early days of the Roman Empire.

In particular, Queen Anne's England was fascinated by the figure of Cicero, whom it perceived as representative of an age to which it likened itself. The great popularity of Middleton's *Life of Cicero*, published in 1741, has been attributed to this sense of identification:

> The story that Middleton had to tell was not only sublime, but also central to the concerns and anxieties that preoccupied a generation constantly comparing itself with classical antiquity, feeling itself to be a free people whose heritage was threatened by factious and corrupt politicians.[1]

Early eighteenth-century England was granted a peculiarly intimate approach to this classical giant through his correspondence. The English Augustans chose to believe that Cicero had unwittingly written his own autobiography in his letters. These letters, characterized by an apparently naked vulnerability of emotion, by numerous passages revelatory of cowardice or self-deception, by the inclusion of petty detail, lent a very human dimension to an eminently 'public' or 'historical' figure. Indeed, on his chancing to discover the manuscripts of Cicero's letters to Atticus, Quintus and Brutus in the Cathedral Library at Verona in 1345, Petrarch wept because they destroyed his idealized notion of Cicero's character.[2]

Middleton had cast his *Life* within the framework of Cicero's letters. Aware that his readers might be disconcerted or ever repelled by the very openness with which Cicero had written them, Middleton cautioned them to place the correspondence in the context of the life:

to form our notions of a great man, from some slight passages of his writings, or separate points of conduct, without regarding their connection with the whole, or the figure, that they make in his general character, is like examining things in a microscope, which were made to be surveyed in the gross.[3]

Middleton also reminded his readers, in the preface, that he had drawn the materials for his work from their proper source, from Cicero himself, whose writings represented the 'most authentic monuments that remain to us, of all the great transactions of that age.'[4]

It is one of the paradoxes of fame that great figures rarely are remembered in quite the light they had anticipated. That Cicero intended, and even intensely longed, to be remembered by posterity is plain in his life and writings. Thus he addressed a letter to the famous historian, Lucceius, imploring him to write an account of his actions and, particularly, of his role in the defeat of the Catiline conspiracy, in these terms: 'I am extreamly **desirous**, and I hope the World can't **blame** me for it, to see my Name made **immortal** in **your** Works.'[5] The irony, of course, is that it was Cicero who immortalized Lucceius by addressing this letter to him. The historian never got around to writing the memoirs Cicero had proposed, and Cicero would undoubtedly have been highly surprised to find that he is best remembered for his letters and that , of all his works, they are the most widely read.

It is because Cicero was unabashedly egotistical, a relentlessly ambitous man, that we are all the more struck by his failure to recognize the literary merit of his own letters. The letter to Lucceius was an anomaly in Cicero's correspondence as one of the rare letters Cicero deliberately wrote as a 'literary' composition.[6] What has been described as the 'rhetorical complexity' of the Ciceronian oratorical style — the hallmark of his formal writings — is notably lacking in his letters, written with easy fluency in the heat of the moment.[7] Cicero justly remarked in a letter to Lucius Pairius Paetus: 'whatever are the subject of my letters, they still speak the language of conversation.'[8]

It is to expediency alone that we owe the invaluable heritage of Cicero's sixteen volumes of *Ad Familiares*. The lack of a proper postal system and the chance that his messenger might be intercepted and the letters damaged or stolen led Tiro, Cicero's favorite freedman, who served as his amanuensis, to adopt the habit of making two fair copies of the letters which had been dictated to him, sending one and keeping the other for reference. Long after Cicero's death, Tiro composed a biography of his master and arranged for the publication of the copies of the letters. Cicero's friend, Atticus, also kept all the letters sent to him, bound in eleven volumes in his library, but his collection was not made public until some hundred years after Cicero's death, when these letters were first mentioned and quoted by Seneca in his *Epistulae Morales.*

Although Cicero, an indefatigable correspondent, had composed his many letters without thought of their ultimate publication, ironically, he was the founder of a tradition of literary letter writing which paid lip-service to 'naturalness' but which actually was bent on the production of letters self-consciously aimed at posterity. Seneca was the first 'disciple' of this tradition. The publication of Cicero's *Letters to Atticus* in 60 A.D. inspired his decision to cast a series of philosophical essays into the epistolary form in *Epistulae Morales.*[9] These are letters 'in form only'; the one hundred and twenty-four epistles to Seneca's friend, Lucilius, who was abroad on imperial service, actually represented the founding of the essay as a literary form.[10]

While Seneca condemned Cicero's letters for their undiscriminating inclusion of apparently insignificant details of the orator's private life, it is the dearth of this minutiae of daily existence which renders his own, considered as letters, vapid and patently artificial. Seneca made a habit of including in each letter, usually towards its close, what he variously described as a 'payment of dues', a 'present', a 'toll', a 'daily stipend', or an 'excellent saying'. These consisted of maxims or quotations garnered from philosophers. That these philosophical 'gifts' were for the use of future generations as well as for Seneca's ostensible correspondent is made plain in Epistle XXI in which Seneca promises Lucilius immortality and in Epistle VIII in which Seneca admits 'I am at work for posterity'.[11]

A generation after Seneca came what has been described as the second great collection of Latin letters, those written by Pliny the younger. Pliny's consciousness of the letter as a literary form and his decision to publish, from time to time, selections from his own correspondence, has been attributed to the continuing popularity of Cicero's letters.[12] Pliny's forte was descriptive narrative, and the elegant, polished tone of his letters accords with his hope that they might be published, an ambition especially transparent in two letters describing the eruption of Vesuvius which Pliny sent to the most famous historian of his age; they are letters in which we can see that Pliny is 'straining every nerve to earn a place for himself in the pages of Tacitus.'[13]

Disingenuousness is the hallmark of the contrived essays both Seneca and Pliny passed off as personal letters. Just as Seneca went so far as to claim that the proper style in letter writing was a kind of 'talking upon paper,' so Pliny made a similar pretence to epistolary naturalness in these letters. The first, a colorful composition complete with dialogue, concludes on a tellingly insincere note:

You will choose out of this narrative such circumstances as shall be most suitable to your purpose; for there is a great difference between what is proper for a letter and an history; between writing to a friend, and writing to the public.[14]

The achievements of the roman letter writers were largely lost sight of until the fourteenth century, when Petrarch chanced upon manuscripts of Cicero's letters. The effect they had on Petrarch tells us something of the interest they were to hold for his own and subsequent ages. On reading the manuscripts, Petrarch was distressed that they revealed a man at odds with the hero he revered, but he was also sufficiently moved to address an open letter to the engagingly fallible personality the letters seemed, unconsciously, to reveal:

I have heard your voice, Cicero, in your copious talk, in your frequent lamentations, in your continual changes; and though I had long known you as an instructor of others, I have now at last discovered what you were in yourself.[15]

According to his biographer, Petrarch's own idea of an epistolarium which he intended to serve as a kind of self-portrait probably was inspired by his discovery of Cicero's letters.[16] Petrarch, like Cicero, composed thousands of letters, but unlike Cicero, he treasured them and fully intended their eventual publication. By 1350 Petrarch's decision to issue an edition of his own letters was a fully-defined project. He divided those in prose into twenty-four books, in imitation of the format of the *Iliad* and the *Odyssey*, beginning the collection with a letter to 'Socrates' and concluding it with a series of letters addressed to his other idols: Cicero, Seneca, Livy, Horace, Virgil and Homer.

Petrarch's letters are moral essays after Seneca's model. Formal literary pieces, they are crowded with quotations from the Roman classics. As his penchant for addressing his letters to classical writers indicates, Petrarch saw his correspondence in the context of an established literary tradition; like Seneca's, it was obviously 'looking beyond the immediate addressee to the ultimate recipient, posterity'.[17] Cicero was Petrarch's inspiration, but Petrarch, like Seneca, relegated the trivial and the mundane and the purely personal to his postscripts, preserving the body of each letter intact in the form of a Latin essay.

Petrarch's immediate successor was Erasmus, who not only adopted a similarly self-conscious attitude toward his own correspondence but went so far as to compose a treatise on letter writing, *De ratione conscribendi epistolas*, published in 1522. Although Erasmus intended his letters to be considered as literature, he managed the deception that they were genuine messages to friends more artfully than had Seneca or Petrarch. He disdained anything approaching artifice or deliberation in their composition, often deprecating his letters. In fact, like Petrarch, Erasmus wrote prolifically, copying and preserving his letters, recalling them from friends and collecting them with a view to publication. He maintained an apparently disinterested role in their being made public by pretending the letters had been stolen from him.[18]

The tradition of unselfconscious literary letter writing is, by its very nature, a contradiction in terms. It has always been conducive to pretension and hypocrisy. While Cicero's example prompted Seneca, Pliny, Petrarch and Erasmus to prepare their own letters for publication, this very element of deliberation robbed their letters, by and large, of the charming air of impulsiveness and the intensely human tone which constitute the prime attraction of Cicero's. In composing essays rather than actual letters, these subsequent aspirants to epistolary fame ironically revealed their failure to comprehend the literary achievement represented by Cicero's own correspondence.

A variety of factors conspired to bring the specifically 'literary' letter intended for publication to prominence and social respectability in eighteenth-century England. These include William Dockwra's founding of the penny post in 1680, accompanied by a corresponding, dramatic increase in the quantity of letters sent to and delivered from all parts of the country, and a rise in literacy, with a new class of shopkeepers, tradesmen and their wives swelling the size of the reading public.

Those who could read must, perforce, wish to write as well. We can posit a 'causal connection' between the penny post and a crop of letter-writer manuals aimed at the new middle class which appeared after 1680.[19] Social and epistolary decorum were taught together in such homely utilitarian formularies as *The Young Secretary's Guide*, which offered model letters entitled 'A Letter from a Serving Man to his Master,' 'A Servant Maid's Letters to her Friends,' and 'A Letter from a Youth to his Father, who is desirous to be bound Apprentice'. The headings of these letters betray their bourgeois bias; they were directed at a class of society 'illiterate' in the Augustan connotation — those who lacked a knowledge of the classical languages and literature.

The age's 'literate' would, as a matter of course, have been exposed at grammar school to the Latin letter writers Cicero, Pliny and Seneca — as well as to Erasmus's treatise on letter writing. 'Polite' society was offered the Roman letter writers as exercises in Latin grammar, composition and translation. The popularity of their published letters, established in the Renaissance, continued strong throughout the eighteenth century, apparent in innumerable editions and translations. A spirit of emulation and even national rivalry was inspired in England, too, by the two immensely popular seventeenth-century French letter writers, Jean Louis Gues de Balzac and Vincent Voiture.

With its potential as the most flexible, versatile and amorphous of literary forms, the letter naturally adapted itself to a wide range of purposes in the eighteenth century. It was used not only to teach etiquette and Latin but also philosophical and theological arguments, political propaganda and travel accounts, real or imaginary, often were cast into the congenial letter form. Four of Pope's closest friends may furnish us with examples, to wit: Arbuthnot delivered his *Essay on the Usefulness of Mathematical Learning* (1701) in a 'Letter from a Gentleman in the City'; Swift preached a powerful political polemic in the *Drapier's Letters* (1724); Bolingbroke analyzed the paucity of good English historical literature in *Letters on the Study and Use of History* (1752); and Lady Mary Wortley Montagu cast a sociological travelogue into epistolary form in her 'Turkish Embassy Letters' (1763).

Richmond Bond distinguishes three types of eighteenth-century letters. First, there was the intimate message intended only for its recipient; second, the more formal 'public' letter designed for a wider audience; and, third, the fictitious letter used as a literary device.[20] But Lady Mary's 'Turkish Embassy Letters', to take but one example, throw into question the usefulness of these three distinctions in describing the sheer diversity of the age's correspondence.

The 'Turkish Embassy Letters', published posthumously, to great acclaim, consists of fifty-two purportedly genuine letters sent by Lady Mary to friends and relations as she accompanied her husband's embassy to Constantinople in 1718. However, subsequent research has shown that the 'Turkish Embassy Letters' actually represent a 'compilation of pseudo-letters' which Lady Mary composed upon her return to England, drawing upon observations jotted down in a daily journal she had kept in Turkey.[21]

Lady Mary's techniques in revising her diary material for publication resembled Pope's editing of his actually letters for that purpose: redating, splicing, and the omission of trivial or intimate detail. The changes were generally minor ones, guided by stylistic consideration. Indeed, when we compare Lady Mary's 'Turkish Embassy Letters' with her actual correspondence, obviously not intended for publication, it is difficult to distinguish between the two. Thus, while the 'Turkish Embassy Letters' fall into Bond's second category, they are sufficiently similar to Lady Mary's genuine personal letters to have been mistaken for such—just as Pope's published letters were.

A number of factors contributed to what we might describe as a certain formality and elegance characteristic of eighteenth-century correspondence. These include the fact that, in that age, the recipient of a letter was expected to pay for its postage; that the letter might contain news or information not accessible elsewhere; and that it was common contemporary practice for a letter to be read aloud to the recipient's family, friends and neighbours. Considering both the importance of the letter as a means of communication at that time and, consequently, the semi-public nature it assumed, it is not surprising that the general custom was to draft a letter and then to copy it out in a fair hand to be sent. In this way, Pope's and Lady Mary's letters, both revised and actual, like most Augustan correspondence, hovered between the first and second of Bond's categories: they were at once private and public.

The practice of making a first draft of their letters led a number of individuals of that period to engage in a peculiarly Augustan form of entertainment: they kept copies of letters they had send collated with letters received and read through them as through a book. Laetitia Pilkington has handed down the famous anecdote of Swift's habit of pasting letters from his friends into a translation of Horace's *Epistles* from which the original pages had been removed.[22] In a letter Richardson sent to a friend in 1755 he admitted that he also engaged in this curious custom; the entertainment and instruction afforded by reading his own correspondence might resemble that which he intended for the audience of his epistolary novels:

> I am employing myself at present, in looking over & sorting, & classing my Correspondencies & other Papers. This, when done, will amuse me by reading over again, a very ample Correspondence: & in comparing the Sentiments of my Correspondents at the time, with their present; & improving from both.[23]

Bond's distinction between fact and fiction, as well as the distinction between letters published for different classes of society, was blurred as early as 1568 when Angel Day succumbed to the impulse to fictionalize and to dramatize letters in his letter-writer manual, *The English Secretorie.* While his predecessors had humbly acknowledged their near total dependence on Latin formularies from which they had transcribed letters for inclusion in their own treatises on epistolography, Day claimed that he had himself composed the form letters in his collection. Breton's *Poste with a Packet of Madde Letters* (1602) carried Day's impulse to its logical conclusion and may be seen as the forerunner of the epistolary novel. Breton's leap from commonsensical advice on writing actual letters to the realm of fiction was, of course, most notably followed by Richardson, for *Pamela* evolved from his epistolary formulary *Familiar Letters on Important Occasions.*

The letter was no less instrumental in the development of the periodical essay. The earliest examples of this distinctively Augustan genre — John Dunton's *Athenian Mercury* (1698) and Defoe's *Advice from the Scandal Club* (1704) — consisted primarily of purportedly real letters from anonymous correspondents printed with responses from the editors: a format they may have deliberately adopted from Breton's popular Poste. The personal letter to the editor became a standard feature of periodical journals, with the *Tatler* and the *Spectator*, combined, including more than eight hundred letters.

It is probable that these popular periodicals stimulated a trend toward self-conscious and deliberately literary letter writing as it was common knowledge that the actual letters submitted to the *Tatler* or the *Spectator* would be revised and polished before publication. In fact, this policy of editorial intervention was encouraged as well as expected. Steele once observed that he felt he 'ought sometimes to lay before the World of plain Letters of [his] Correspondents in the artless Dress' in which they had been sent, but that his editorial assistance was expressly requested by his readers.[24]

There is a curious discrepancy on this point between Augustan profession and practice. Pope's early mentor William Walsh uttered a popular eighteenth-century maxim in the preface of his *Letters and Poems* (1692): 'The style of letters ought to be free, easy, and natural: as near approaching to familiar conversation as possible.'[25] But in their letters the Augustans always aimed at the simplicity and naturalness of individuals in whom the values of a highly-civilized society had been inculcated. They would have been horrified had they actually encountered in their correspondence the colloquial or the random discourse which might realistically approximate their oft-expressed belief that the perfect epistolary style must resemble intimate discourse.

If the preferred Augustan epistolary style was a kind of 'talking on paper' (a figure enthusiastically appropriated from Seneca), the preferred content of the eighteenth-century letter was its author's 'heart'. The age was fond of the image, adapted from Lucian's *Hermotimus*, of the letter as a kind of 'window in the bosom' through which the writer's most private thoughts and feelings might be rendered visible. In the mid-seventeenth century Thomas Forde, in his *Faenestra in Pectore*, made one of the first explicit references to this classical notion, explaining the title of his letter collection in these terms:

The witty *Lucian* brings in *Momus,* quarreling at the Master-pieces which the *gods* had made; and the onley fault he found with *Man,* was, *That he had not a window to look into his breast.* For this reason, I call this *Packet* of *Letters Fenestra in Pectore.* Letters being the best *Casements,* whereby men disclose themselves.[26]

The ramifications of this popular concept of the familiar letter as a kind of 'window in the bosom' included the belief that only a letter written without publication in mind would provide this view of its author's true character; that its style naturally would approximate 'talking on paper'; and that the published letters of famous individuals might serve as useful moral instruction. This latter belief had been adopted from the humanist tradition, which sought to teach morality by capturing readers' imaginations with 'lessons through lives,' thereby giving a 'vividly conceived ideal of what [man] ought to be, along with certain precepts about how to approach that ideal.'[27]

The humanists felt that the classical writers had bequeathed, in the form of their correspondence, either valuable historical documents, as in the case of Cicero's letters, or a body of moral philosophy, as in the case of Seneca's. It was felt, too, that moral or historical lessons delivered in the medium of the letter might be more intelligible or affecting than when those lessons were divorced from the human context or, as Seneca once observed, the 'way by precept is long and tedious; whereas that of example is short and powerful.'[28]

The unselfconscious nature of Cicero's letters, in particular, exerted a powerful influence on the Augustan imagination, for these letters seemed to prove that a great man might, unintentionally, write his own biography in the form of his correspondence. Pope's friend Bolingbroke put his finger on their special attraction for his age in his observation that, while Pliny, Seneca, Balzac and Voiture had apparently written their letters for the public,

> Tully did not, and therefore these give us more pleasure than any which have come down to us from Antiquity. When we read them, we pry into a Secret which was intended to be kept from us . . . We see Cato, and Brutus, and Pompey and others, such as they really were.[29]

The eighteenth century early established and consistently maintained a link between the familiar letter and moral instruction. The most famous proponent of this connection, Richardson, expressed his belief in the didactic potential of the epistolary form in his earliest letter, which he recalled having sent to a hypocritical widow who 'pretending to a Zeal for Religion, & who was a constant Frequenter of Church Ordinances, was continually fomenting Quarrels & Disturbances, by Backbiting & Scandal, among all her Acquaintance.'[30] But there were notable epistolary 'missionaries' before Richardson, foremost among them, Addison and Steele, who aimed in their periodicals to educate the new middle class's morals as well as manners, to 'recommend truth, innocence, honour, and virtue, as the chief ornaments of life.'[31]

The middle class's interest in gossip about the great figures of the age and 'polite' society's interest in humanist 'lessons through lives' were simultaneously gratified by biography set within the framework of personal letters. Interest in the 'history' of famous persons could be turned to good use if the biography offered an example of a life worthy of imitation for, as Curll once pointed out, the lessons to be derived from biography often proved more 'lively and affecting' than those imparted by moral precepts.

But the English aspirants to epistolary fame were hindered by the same tacit taboo which had perplexed Pliny and Seneca, Petrarch and Erasmus. The publication of familiar letters in the eighteenth century was still an unusual occurrence, and 'grave doubts were entertained as to the delicacy and propriety of such a proceeding.'[32] It was only permissable to publish personal correspondence posthumously, and only if it consisted of letters of state or of recognized official or historical interest.

What was not allowed was than an individual should deliberately set out to publish his own letters. The Augustan letter writer wanting to print his own thus was forced to engage in a number of ploys to avoid the controversy such publications inspired in his age. He could attempt, as Lady Mary did, to ensure that his correspondence would be published posthumously. He might, like Wycherley, Dryden, Walsh, Dennis and Congreve, openly imitate the French epistolary models and print his letters in classical and continental letter collections. He might, like Arbuthnot, Swift and Bolingbroke, renounce all claim to epistolary naturalness in the essays he published in the letter form. Or he might, like Pope, follow the example of Erasmus, and pretend that his letters had been stolen from him.

On the one hand, popular recognition of the letter as a literary genre inspired the achievements of a number of the greatest artists in the form, resulting in the eighteenth century's often being dubbed the 'age of the great English Letter Writers'. On the other, 'letters were still considered private communications and to publish one's own was a breach of taste.'[33] The Augustans' paradoxical attitude is well illustrated by Lord Orrery in his *Life* of Swift. First, Lord Orrery repeated the commonplace that 'no part of an author's writings give a greater insight into his natural disposition than his letters,' and then, unaware of any contradiction, he deplored the pernicious 'licence which of late has too much prevailed of publishing epistolary correspondences.'[34] The final irony, of course, is that these observations were made in the context of a biography consisting of a series of letters Lord Orrery supposedly sent is son, Hamilton.

CHAPTER THREE

Pope as Augustan Letter Writer

The letter was a peculiarly appropriate literary genre for Pope in both his public and his private capacities. Afflicted at age twelve by Pott's disease, the letter offered the fragile poet, often invalided by headache and fever, an invaluable, irreplaceable way to keep in touch with his friends. Similarly, Pope maintained contact with his reading public and with the world at large by means of the poetic epistle, issued from his rural seclusion in Twickenham. In his youth, Pope was famous for the 'ramble', but from 1717 to 1735, following his father's death, he minimized his travels, believing his mother 'grown too feeble to be left long alone'.[1] Ill health and a strong sense of filial duty, then, left Pope heavily dependent on the letter. Too, although this prohibition was rarely enforced, the Catholics of the early eighteenth century were still bound by a number of penal laws and, in Pope's lifetime, they were twice banished from London in the government's fears of a Jacobite invasion. All these circumstances provided an impetus for Pope's establishing and maintaining a vast network of friendships and contacts sustained almost entirely through correspondence.

Apart from its obvious usefulness as a means through which 'friends disjoin'd may correspond and greet', (no inconsiderable matter for Pope, whose intimates, Swift and Bolingbroke, were in exile from England for the greater part of their friendship), Pope turned to the letter as a medium through which he could express himself with greater ease and skill than the informality of actual discourse allowed. In his *Life* of Pope Dr. Johnson observed that, like Dryden, this poet did not 'excel' in 'familiar or convivial conversation'.[2] Lord Chesterfield, too, believed that, in speaking, Pope was 'below himself; he was seldom easy and natural, and seemed afraid that the man should degrade the poet, which made him always attempt wit and humour, often unsuccessfully, and too often unseasonably'.[3] Pope, morbidly sensitive about his physical shortcomings, keenly anxious to preserve his dignity as the foremost poet of his age, naturally found the letter, written in privacy, amenable to revision and amendment, often preferable for the expression of his ideas to the pressures and demands of face-to-face conversation.

Pope could scarcely escape an awareness of the letter as an important literary genre, as a means of expression perhaps as distinctively Augustan as the herioc couplet. Pope's earliest friends contributed to this awareness as nearly all of them were involved in letter publications. The prominent critic Walsh who, upon reading Pope's *Pastorals*, adopted him as a literary protégé, was closely connected with the literary letter in England, publishing *Letters and Poems* in 1692. Walsh prefaced this work with an interesting defence of the age's predilection for publishing letters, observing that the belief that 'familiar Letters can please none, but those very Persons [to whom they have been directed], is to conclude against the common Experience of all the World.'[4]

Most of Pope's other early friends concurred with Walsh's calm assurance that personal letters can interest an audience wider than their intended recipients. A 1696 edition of *Letters Upon Several Occasions* had included among its contributors not only Pope's self-confessed literary model, Dryden, but also the man who was to become his arch enemy, John Dennis, as well as two of Pope's earliest, most distinguished acquaintances, Wycherley and Congreve. In 1700 these same individuals collaborated with another of Pope's early friends and correspondents, the minor critic and poet, Henry Cromwell, on a translation of Voiture's *Familiar Letters*.

The two times the admiring Wycherley threatened to publish his youthful correspondent's precociously clever letters to him must have reminded Pope of Wycherley's involvement in *Letters Upon Several Occasions*. In the first instance, Wycherley claimed his own letters had been included in this publication, edited by Dennis, without his knowledge or consent; in the second, Wycherley openly warned 'I will revenge the raillery of your Letters upon mine, by printing them, (as *Dennis* did mine) **without your knowledge too.**'[5]

From the evidence provided by his own letters, it is obvious that Pope was well-versed in the epistolary models, classical and continental, popular in his own age. Pope was especially fond of quoting Seneca who is, with Cicero, Pliny, Balzac and Voiture, the subject of a lengthy debate carried on by Pope, Swift and Bolingbroke in their own correspondence over which of these famous figures had actually written his letters with an eye to their ultimate publication.[6]

Throughout his letter-writing career Pope readily adapted to changing epistolary fashions. In his youth he enthusiastically adopted the 'precious' style of his earliest distinguished correspondents, Wycherley, Walsh and Cromwell. With an accuracy bordering on parody Pope managed to capture the tone and imagery of his friends' letters: the elaborate flattery and hyperbole inherited from Voiture and Balzac coupled with the indecorous wit of a Restoration comedy. The hallmark of the 'precious' letter was the ingenious conceit or the ironic compliment. In *Letters Upon Several Occasions*, for example, Dennis addressed Wycherley in the approved style by remarking, 'I am as reasonable with my Friend, as a **Russian** spouse is with her Husband, and take his very Railery for a mark of Esteem, as she does a Beating for a proof of Affection.'[7] With his infallible talent for mimicry, Pope softened the misogyny of this idea in a letter to Cromwell: 'As the fooling and toying with a mistress is a proof of fondness, not disrespect, so is raillery with a friend.'[8]

But the 'courtly' style advocated by these early correspondents was rapidly waning in popularity even as Pope so skilfully adopted it. The turn of the century witnessed a dramatic shift in epistolary fashions, largely attributable to the growth of the new middle class, which rejected the rhetorical extravagances of the 'precious' style in favor of a simple, clear, easy style in letters. However, we must remember that the Augustan notion of language as a function and measure of civilization precluded the development of a truly casual or conversational epistolary style.

Pope's first allusion to the popular notion of the ideal epistolary style as a kind of 'talking upon paper' was contained in a letter he sent to Wycherley in 1710. Like his contemporaries, Pope drew a direct correlation between a letter's style and content, remarking in 1712 that:

> you see my letters are scribbled with all the carelessness and inattention imaginable: my style, like my soul, appears in its natural undress before my friend.[9]

In 1720, rather disingenuously, Pope rebuked Lady Hervey for what he condemned as affectation and artificiality in her letters to him, singling out his old model Voiture in his criticism:

> Now let me fairly tell you, I don't like your style: 'tis very pretty, therefore I don't like it; and if you writ as well as Voiture, I wou'd not give a farthing for such letters, unless I were to sell 'em to be printed.[10]

In fact, the claims Pope increasingly made in his later letters to informality, to 'throwing out his self upon paper' without caution or reserve, were justified only in those letters he addressed to John Caryll, a fellow Catholic, one of Pope's closest friends and perhaps his most faithful correspondent. Caryll and Pope met in 1710 and began a correspondence which lasted without intermission (excepting a brief period in 1716) until Caryll's death in 1736. Pope's frankness and ease in his letters to Caryll is probably attributable to the fact that theirs was not a friendship based primarily on literary interests. Pope and Caryll shared a concern with 'practical Christianity', and their letters are largely taken up with discussion of the various charities and philanthropical projects they engaged in and on which they often collaborated.

Pope's youthful fondness for ingenious conceits, elaborate metaphors and rakish wit was relinquished in even his earliest letters to Caryll. But the tendency toward writing on moralistic or philosophical matters was latent also in Pope's letters to Cromwell or Wycherley, in which he often, abruptly, dropped the pose of the worldly man-about-town to assume a persona perhaps more natural to him: the dutiful son conveying his parents' good wishes to his friends or inviting them to the family home at Binfield.

Sobering reflections on mortality and, as Pope perceived it, its concomitant, morality, were never far from Pope's mind. His early acquaintance with serious illness led him 'in boyhood to notify his friends of his approaching demise.'[11] Pope was also influenced by Addison and Steele, and their philosophy, as expressed in the *Tatler* and *Spectator* papers, that 'wit, if a man had it, unless it be directed to some useful end, is but a wanton frivolous quality' anticipated Pope's belief that 'No writing is good that does not tend to better mankind some way or other.'[12]

Pope saw no incongruity in his abrupt shift from the excesses of *préciosité* to the sermonizing which characterized the letters of his maturer years, when in his correspondence as well as in his poetry he had 'stoop'd to Truth, and moraliz'd his song.' While, in his youth, Pope greatly admired what he described as Voiture's ability to 'write agreably upon Triffles,' Seneca came to exert the greatest epistolary influence on Pope, who adopted the habit of quoting from the *Epistulae Morales* in his own letters. In one to his friend Robert Digby, for example, Pope abstracted one of Seneca's useful philosophic 'gems' to describe his sense of loss at the death of a neighbour: 'Nothing, says **Seneca**, is so melancholy a circumstance in human Life, or so soon reconciles us to the thought of our own death, as the reflection and prospect of one Friend after another dropping round us!'[13]

Because Pope's despised religion and poor health meant he was a man 'born to retirement perforce,' Pope had quite deliberately to fashion an image of himself in his writings to set before his friends and his public.[14] This persona naturally evolved as Pope himself matured and, thus, we find the mischievous would-be rake who corresponded with Wycherley and Cromwell is gradually replaced by a man conscious of the dignity of his position as the most important writer of his age. To his 'inferiors' Pope used the letter to deliver pronouncements *ex cathedra*; to his 'equals', and in letters to the Scriblerians in particular, we find Pope a self-consciously clever correspondent.

Acutely sensitive to current literary trends, Pope appropriated the popular metaphor his contemporaries had adopted from Lucian and made it the topic of a letter he sent Lady Mary in 1716:

> If Momus his project had taken of having Windows in our breasts, I should be for carrying it further and making those windows Casements: that while a Man showd his Heart to all the world, he might do something more for his friends, e'en take it out, and trust it to their handling.[15]

This image reappears in 1720 in a letter to his friend Charles Jervas, the painter: 'The old project of a Window in the bosom, to render the Soul of Man visible, is what every honest friend has manifold reason to wish for.'[16]

In his early years, Pope was not only impressing his elderly friends with his precocious epistolary genius in private letters; he was also already practising writing essays cast into the letter form for publication. It has been established that Pope authored at least three such essays for the *Spectator* in 1712, and nine other *Spectator* papers are generally attributed to him. In the first *Guardian* in volume form, Steele ascribed six papers, first published in 1713, to Pope, and an additional eight were possibly also contributed by him.[17]

These contributions followed the contemporary pattern in consisting of essays 'written to no one in particular' but which took the form of the personal letter addressed to the journal's editor. Pope's anonymous letters often took Pope himself as their subject; his letter in *Spectator* 527, for example, was devoted to an appraisal of his own poem *On a Fan*. Of the nine *Spectator* papers generally attributed to Pope, 316 is of particular interest in its reflecting the author's familiarity with classical letter writers and his Augustan habit of turning to them for instruction and entertainment:

> All are acquainted with the Labour and Assiduity with which **Tully** acquired his Eloquence. **Seneca** in his letters to **Lucelius** assures him, there was not a Day in which he did not either write something, or read and epitomize some good Author; and I remember **Pliny** in one of his Letters, where he gives an Account of the various Methods he used to fill up every Vacancy of Time, after several Imployments, which he enumerates.[18]

Of the eight additional *Guardian* papers describes as 'with much probability' written by Pope, 106 and 172 are, for the present purpose, the most interesting.[19] *Guardian* 106 recounts the story of Momus who 'is said to have found Fault with the Make of a Man, because he had not a Window in his Breast,' a tale whose moral is that 'the Heart of Man is so full of Wiles and Artifices, Treachery and Deceit, that there is no guessing at what he is from his Speeches and outward Appearance.'[20] Lucian's story reappears in *Guardian* 172, an essay on the origin and use of letters, which are accorded the function of serving as this 'window in the bosom':

> The Philosopher who wish'd he had a Window to his Breast, to lay open his Heart to all the World, might as easily have reveal'd the Secrets of it this way, and as easily left them to the World, as wish'd it. This silent Art of speaking by Letters, remedies the Inconvenience arising from distance of Time, as well as Place.[21]

The author of *Guardian* 172, then, perceived letters as of particular value as a means not only of transcending the limitations of time and space but also of surmounting the hurdle of mortality itself. Letters allow one to 'correspond with a Friend at a distance, or . . . to take the Opinion of an Honest Gentleman, who has been dead this thousand Years.' The art of letter writing 'preserves the Works of the Immortal part of Men, so as to make the Dead still useful to the Living.'

If, by and large, Pope was very much a letter writer of his age, echoing its commonplaces and conventions, his correspondence is anomalous in one important respect: its indifference to current affairs. While his contemporaries' letters are preoccupied by news, and by politics in particular, Pope's letters, like Jane Austen's novels, reflect little awareness of a world existing beyond the private circle of family and friends. In his early 'letters of wit', Pope seemed deliberately to follow Voiture's example in treating news ironically, delivering it whimsically, with mock-gravity. In his subsequent, moralistic letters he used news merely as a brief departure point for entry into timeless philosophizing. Pope seemed to feel that it was beneath his dignity as a writer to concern himself with day-to-day events. This, at least, is hinted at in a letter he sent the Blount sisters in 1715, in which he complains at their request for news, claiming this reduces him to a 'Brother of Dyer & Dawkes,' two Grub Street hacks.[22]

In addition to Pope's unwillingness to descend in his writing to mere journalism, it is likely that those very physical and social constraints which contributed to make the letter a genre invaluable for Pope in communicating with his friends and his public also played a large part in determining the nature of his correspondence. Apart from a letter of 1740 Pope was prompted to address to Lord Marchmont, urging him to enlist in Bolingbroke's Opposition to Walpole's government, his correspondence is characterized by a neutrality remarkable in an age of turbulent political and religious controversy. Practical considerations, of course, underlay this avoidance of partisanship, particularly in view of Pope's Catholicism, but this expediency was also simply a fortunate circumstance for

Pope, whose favored epistolary, as opposed to poetical, themes inclined toward the philosophical and the psychological rather than the topical or the historical.[23]

Pope was always more interested in what his correspondents thought and felt than in what they saw or did. Although his delicate health deprived him of the opportunity to travel on the continent, he was impatient with the travelogues Lady Mary insisted on sending him en-route with her husband to Turkey. 'For Gods sake Madam,' Pope declared in a letter of 1716, 'when you write to me, talk of your self, there is nothing I so much desire to hear of . . . The Shrines and Reliques you tell me of, no way engage my curiosity.'[24] In 1735 Pope asserted that the letter's primary value lay in its potential as an expression of friendship, as he observed in a letter to Mrs. Knight:

> Madam, — I must keep my old custom of giving my friends now and then, once or twice a year, my testimony in writing that I love and esteem them . . . I have never any thing else to say, and it is all that friend ship and good-will can, or ought to say: the rest is only matter of curiosity, which a newspaper can better gratify.[25]

Not surprisingly, Pope's favorite topic in his own letters was himself. His early letters are full of requests that his correspondents either criticize his work or analyze his character. In 1712 Pope requested Caryll to return his letters, believing, apparently, that they might serve as a treasury of ideas and phrases he might re-use in writing articles for the *Spectator* and *Guardian*. Considering the extensiveness of their correspondence, Caryll was an obvious choice for what Pope termed this 'odd request'; some 150 letters passed between him and Pope from 1710 to 1736. While it has been posited that Pope did 'borrow' from these letters, the recalled correspondence also proved to hold an unsuspected value and attraction for Pope, who subsequently enthused to Caryll that it was as though, like Cicero, he had managed unwittingly to write his own 'story' in his letters:

> Upon a review of them I find many things that would give me shame, if I were not more desirous to be thought honest than prudent; so many things freely thrown out, such lengths of unreserved friendship, thought just warm from the brain without any polishing or dress, the very **déshabille** of the understanding.[26]

Pope regarded the correspondence recalled from Caryll as an intriguing, involuntarily intimate projection of himself; rereading it was an exercise at once humbling and flattering, as he observed to Caryll: 'You have at length complied with the request I have often made to you; for you have shown me I must confess several of my faults in the light of those letters.'[27] As Ault and James Winn have conjectured, Pope obviously perceived these letters as 'raw material' not only for 'literature' but also for 'self-examination.'[28]

Pope's interest in his own letters might have remained confined to a purely personal level had Curll not published, in 1726, an unauthorized collection of his letters to Henry Cromwell. Pope was undoubtedly embarrassed by the sudden appearance of these early letters: chagrined by their revelations of his youthful vanity, by the pedantic, long-winded literary debates and the indecorous wit which had characterized his correspondence with Cromwell. But he was also probably gratified by their popularity, for this publication had more than an 'ephemeral success'; in 1729 Curll gleefully observed that it was still selling well.[29]

As Pope's unsympathetic Victorian editor, Elwin, surmised, it is probable that the popularity of this publication led Pope to thoughts of issuing more of his letters. The Homer manuscripts, consisting of the backs of letters and envelopes which this 'paper-sparing' poet had used as scrap material on which to translate the *Iliad* represent irrefutable evidence that, in the years 1713-19, Pope was not 'saving' letters.[30] But from 1726 onwards we find Pope making increasingly frequent, increasingly pressing requests that his correspondents return his letters. As Pope had grown somewhat estranged from Caryll by this time, it proved more difficult to persuade him to accede to this request; possibly Caryll wanted to retain them as a testimonial of his former intimacy with the great poet. In December 1726 Pope promised he would review any letters Caryll sent him and to

> return whatever can do no hurt to either of us, or our memories, or to any other particular man's character; but so much, as would serve to bear testimony of my own love for good men, or theirs for me.[31]

The letters were returned to Pope shortly after he sent a second imploring request to Caryll in 1727, although Pope was unaware that Caryll had instructed his daughter to copy them before returning the original letters.

In the period 1726-36 Pope also requested the return of his old letters from the widow of his former correspondent, Edward Blount, and from such current correspondents as Hugh Bethel, Lord Digby, William Fortescue, Joseph Spence, Swift, and from Broome.[32] He had more success with some of these applications than with others. His letters to Swift, for example, were returned only after a prolonged struggle, and Broome simply refused. Some of his old correspondents had, like Lady Mary Wortley Montagu, become his enemies or, like Caryll, estranged from him. Executors proved a prime source of letters.[33] Although Pope's own health was exceedingly precarious, as a precocious young poet he had cultivated the friendship of many individuals much older than himself: Walsh had died in 1708, Wycherley and Trumbull in 1716, Parnell in 1718, Addison in 1719, James Craggs in 1721, Digby and Blount in 1726, Cromwell in 1728, Steele and Congreve in 1729, Gay in 1732 and Arbuthnot in 1735.

By whatever means he retrieved them, by 1729 Pope had amassed a sufficient number to engage in a habit also indulged in by Swift and Richardson, of intercalating his own letters with those of his correspondents in the form of a book. In a letter to Caryll of that year Pope observed: 'Some of my own letters have been returned to me, which I have put into order with theirs; and it makes all together an unimportant, indeed, but yet an innocent history of myself.' On this occasion, Pope found it a more gratifyingly unblemished self-portrait than he had seventeen years earlier, and he spoke to Swift of the enjoyment he derived from perusing this volume, produced

> for my own secret satisfaction, in reviewing a Life, past in Innocent amusements & Studies, not without the good will of worthy and ingenious Men.[34]

In 1729 Pope began preparing his recalled letters for deposit in Lord Oxford's Harleian Library as a first step toward their ultimate, seemingly disinterested publication. But Pope's habit of sending carefully-wrought prose pieces to a number of correspondents suggests that, quite early on, Pope regarded his letters in a special way. Besides the 'psychological' letter taking himself as its subject, Pope was also fond of composing descriptive narratives after the fashion of Pliny, and he adopted a habit of sending such 'set pieces' to a number of correspondents. A dramatic tale of two rural lovers killed by lighting while sheltering from a storm in a haystack, for example, was sent to Martha Blount, in collaboration with Gay, to either Fortescue or Fenton and to Lord Bathurst, to an unsympathetic Lady Mary, and eventually to Caryll and Atterbury.[35] Similarly, he sent an extensive description of Stanton Harcourt, which he described as a 'true picture of a genuine Ancient Country Seat' to both Lady Mary and the Duke of Buckingham. Pope apparently quickly arrived at a view of his letters as literary constructs midway between publishable essays and actual private letters.

This special attitude towards his letters may have arisen in part from Pope's numerous collaborations with Gay on letters to mutual friends. Pope also wrote a letter with Lady Mary in 1716 and collaborated with Bolingbroke on a number of letters to Swift. In 1714 the Scriblerians had collaborated on rhymed notes to an invitation to the Earl of Oxford; this habit of sending letters to which each member had contributed a paragraph or a verse reached its culmination in the famous 1726 'Cheddar' letter which Pope, Gay, Bolingbroke, Mrs. Howard, Pulteney and Arbuthnot sent to Swift.

Pope's correspondence is remarkable for the fact that expressions, phrases and figures of speech reappear again and again through both the original and the revised letters. From 1718 until his mother's death in 1733, for example, Pope habitually likened her uncertain health to the evanescence of a dying candle. If Pope was not averse to repeating himself in his letters—a habit which must have hovered between the deliberate and the unintentional—neither was he loath to extract phrases from the letters he had been sent for inclusion in his own. In 1724, for example, he apparently pilfered a number of sentences from a letter he had just received from the Earl of Oxford and passed them off as his own in a letter he was writing to Lady Newsham.[36]

Pope obviously failed to make any distinction between his public and his private writings, between letters that he sent to friends and formal literary pieces that he carefully crafted for his reading public. Similarly, it was his habit to re-use any material, in whatever form it had first appeared, as the need arose. As we have seen, Pope hoped to cannibalize the thoughts and phrases appearing in his original letters to Caryll in composing submissions to the *Spectator* and the *Guardian*. His contributions to these popular periodical journals were derived from a variety of sources and, in their turn, served as source material for subsequent literary projects. An examination of *Spectator* 404, for example, yields more than twelve points of comparison between Pope's essay on affectation and such other works as a letter to Wycherley of 1705, the *Essay on Criticism*, a *Guardian* submission and the *Essay on Man*. Norman Ault is inclined to link this paper with the *Essay on Criticism* in particular, observing that 'not a little of [it] may be said to furnish prose illustrations and more or less close paraphrases of parts' of that poem.[37] Pope was able to abstract not only ideas but also particular phrases from earlier works for inclusion in his periodical papers or his letters or his poems. A letter to Cromwell of 1708 apparently furnished phrases for *Spectator* papers 316 and 406. Spectator 292 contains a phrase Pope had coined two years earlier in the *Essay on Criticism*: ' . . . in each/Are *nameless Graces* which no Methods teach' is transformed in this paper into 'The one is full of numberless nameless Graces.'[38]

While vanity—a desire to demonstrate his considerable epistolary skill as well as to advertise his intimacy with the great figures of his age—

played its part in Pope's decision to publish his correspondence, we may also see Pope as letter writer as one of Seneca's heirs. In both his *Moral Essays* and in his published letters Pope appealed to humanist tradition in seeking to present a tale which taught by example. As we will see in the next chapter, Pope did not fundamentally alter the sense of his letters in revising them for publication. Rather, his concern was to offer a somewhat idealized if generally comprehensible portrait of a group of remarkable individuals. From a perception of his recalled letters as comprising a pleasingly unselfconscious autobiography and, intercalated with those of his correspondents, as a history of himself and his friends, Pope gradually arrived at the belief that, published, these letters might serve as an instructive, elevating example of the moral life led by a famous poet and his circle of intimates. Perhaps he hoped that future ages might enthuse over his letters as, echoing received opinion, John Donne had, over those of the great writers of antiquity:

> What treasures of Morall knowledge are in **Senecaes** Letters to onely one **Lucilius**? and what of Naturall in **Plinies**? how much of the stories of the time, is in **Ciceroes** Letters? . . . where can we finde so perfect a Character of **Phalaris**, as in his own letters.[39]

CHAPTER FOUR

The Self-Portrait in the Letters

Traditionally the issue of Pope's publication of his own letters has been used as a stick to beat the poet for what critics have perceived as his duplicity and vanity. A more fruitful approach is suggested by Geoffrey Tillotson, who observes that the first edition of Pope's letters, published in May 1735, appeared at a crucial time in Pope's career: 'his war with the dunces had left him sorer and shabbier than was comfortable'.[1]

The implications of this observation have never been sufficiently assessed. While it is a commonplace that acquaintance with the pamphlet attacks on Pope's character and writings leads one to a greater appreciation of his mature poetry—and especially of the *Dunciad*, the *Moral Essays* and the *Imitations of Horace*—the fact that this applies with equal if not greater force to the letters Pope published has been largely ignored: a surprising omission in studies dealing with Pope's letters.

We know that, despite his cultivated pose of indifference, Pope was acutely affected by the hundreds of poems and essays published by Grub Street in an effort to destroy his personal and poetical reputation. Dr. Johnson has left us, of course, the most famous anecdotal account:

> I have heard Mr. Richardson relate that he attended his father the painter on a visit, when one of Cibber's pamphlets came into the hands of Pope, who said, 'These things are my diversion'. They sat by him while he perused it, and saw his features writhen with anguish; and young Richardson said to his father, when they returned, that he hoped to be preserved from such diversion as had been that day the lot of Pope.[2]

Dr. Johnson's story reflects Pope's curiously ambivalent response to the pamphlet attacks: he was both fascinated and tormented by them. The pamphlet warfare could not simply be ignored. Although 'paper wars' were an integral feature of the Augustan literary scene, Pope was the most maligned writer of his age. As Guerinot points out, 'it is, indeed, hard to think of any other figure in English literature who was so frequently attacked in his lifetime'.[3]

Pope's preoccupation with the satire directed against him is most strikingly illustrated by the fact that he collected a great number of these pamphlet attacks, bound them in four volumes, and stored them in his library.[4] On the one hand, Pope simply relished satirical literature, and he was particularly intrigued by the public images of Alexander Pope as the age's foremost poet circulated by both his admirers and detractors. On the other, Pope's collection of the attacks was a somewhat masochistic exercise. He could not help but be deeply pained by the scurrilous nature of the generality of these pamphlets.

John Dennis's *Reflections Critical and Satyrical* on the *Essay on Criticism*, published in 1711, inaugurated the hostilities between Grub Street and Pope and may serve as an example. The material is familiar but bears repeating; it is, indeed, possible to categorize the criticisms contained in Dennis's *Remarks* as representative because of a curious characteristic of the pamphlet attacks: an accusation against Pope, once printed, acquired the plausibility of truth and was repeated without question, let alone need for confirmation, in subsequent pamphlets.

Remarks is first typical of the many pamphlets for which it served as a model in its sense of injury out of all proportion to the offence it addressed. Dennis's thirty pages of bitter, implacable invective ostensibly were inspired by Pope's unwise but scarcely malicious description of the critic in his *Essay* as an irascible 'Appius'. Pope's epithet proved only too apt. Dennis was legendary for a sensitivity bordering on paranoia, which sensed injury where none was intended. This sensitivity unluckily did not extend to compassion for a twenty-three year old fledgling poet crippled physically by Pott's disease and socially by his allegiance to a despised religion.

Thus the disproportionate sense of grievance in Dennis's pamphlet is accompanied by numerous references to Pope's physical shortcomings, reducing his *Remarks* and most successive pamphlets to the level of crude personal libel. Dennis usually likened Pope to a monkey, but here he attributed Pope's propensity for writing satire to his resemblance to another kind of being: 'As there is no Creature in Nature so venomous, there is nothing so stupid and impotent as a hunch-back'd Toad'. Dennis's fondness for describing Pope in terms of animal imagery led him to question whether the poet should even be considered human. He concluded that Pope's parents must have wished to abort such a 'monster' and that Pope

> had reason to thank the good Gods that he was born a Modern. For had he been born of **Graecian** Parents, and his Father by consequency had by Law had the absolute Disposal of him, his Life had been no longer than that of one of his Poems, the Life of half a day.

Another element of *Remarks* typical of subsequent pamphlets was its attack on Pope's religion. Pope's surname and Catholicism were unfortunate circumstances in an age with a morbid dread of a Jacobite invasion (and which witnessed one in Pope's lifetime). Dennis was only the first of many to accuse Pope of treason. Complaining that Pope's *Essay* had obliquely libelled William of Orange and Charles III in particular and the Dutch in general, he asserted that

> he who Libels our Confederates, must be by Politicks a **Jacobite**; and he who Libels all the Protestant Kings that we have had in this Island these threescore Years . . . is, I suppose, politickly setting up for Poet-Laureat against the coming over of the Pretender, which by his Insolence he seems to believe approaching.

Dennis's *Remarks* again anticipated many subsequent pamphlet attacks on Pope in its accusation that Pope's friendships were largely compounded, on the poet's part, of opportunism and ingratitude. Describing, for example, Pope's intimacy with William Wycherley as a form of parasitism, Dennis commented:

> It has been observ'd that of late Years a certain Spectre exactly in the shape of that little Gentleman, has haunted a certain ancient Wit, and has been by the People of **Covent-Garden** styl'd his evil Genius.

Also generated here was a particularly persistent, damaging rumor which claimed that Pope not only clung to the great dramatist to achieve his own entrée to the great but also that he had gone so far as to compose a poem praising his own *Pastorals* which he had later, audaciously, attributed to the ingenuous Wycherley:

> by this wise Proceeding [Pope] had the Benefit of the Encomium, and Mr. **W—** had the Scandal of the Poetry; which it brought upon him to such a degree, that 'tis ten to one if ever he recovers the Reputation of a good Versifier.

But Pope's other early great friends were not quite so gullible, Dennis hinted, and went on to claim that William Walsh had allowed Pope to accompany him on occasion only as a sort of joke:

> I remember a little young Gentleman, with all the Qualifications which we have found to be in this Author, whom Mr. **Walsh** us'd sometimes to take into his Company as a double Foil to his Person, and his Capacity.[5]

Time and malice honed these daggers hurled at Pope's reputation to a finer cutting edge and added a few more charges to the list. By 1716 Dennis had turned from crude taunting of Pope's physical defects to criticism on a metaphysical plane; in that year he issued a *True Character of Pope* which pronounced, with a solemn air of Biblical injunction, that

> the Deformity of this Libeller is Visible, Present, Lasting, Unalterable, and Peculiar to Himself. 'Tis the mark of God and Nature upon him, to give us

warning that we should hold no Society with him, as a Creature not of our Original, nor of our Species.[6]

By 1733 Lady Mary Wortley Montagu's sense of enmity was strong enough for her to concur and, in verses addressed *To the Imitator Of The Second Book of Horace*, she advised Pope to follow the model of his Biblical ancestor:

> And with the Emblem of thy crooked Mind,
> Mark'd on thy Back, like **Cain**, by God's own Hand,
> Wander, like him, accursed through the Land.[7]

The most popular 'new' charge appearing in pamphlets after Dennis's *Remarks* was that Pope had become a rich man. Indeed, it has often been observed that what Pope's 'dunces' found really unforgiveable about him was his financial success and consequent literary independence of the professional writer's traditional bondage to patronage. Pope represented a literary landmark as the first English writer freed from the old necessity to flatter and to scheme and, although his motives may have been selfish ones, he revolutionized the position of the man of letters in society.[8]

But despite his wealth and prestige, Pope was unable to ignore the pamphlet attacks. His original or, at least, avowed intention had been to maintain a stoical silence. In 1711 he remarked in a letter to his close friend John Caryll that he would not make the

> least reply to [Dennis], not only because you advise me, but because I've ever been of opinion that if a book can't answer for its self to the public, 'tis no sort of purpose for its author to do it.

Swift, too, advised Pope not to 'answer' his detractors, warning him that, like Virgil, he would only succeed in immortalizing his enemies in his verse. But Pope's good intentions and his friends' counsel were overthrown by his naïve belief that his *Dunciad* might 'rid [him] of those insects'.[9]

On one level the *Dunciad*, with its appendix of *A List of Books and Verses, in which our Author was Abused*— including thirty-four items derived from the pamphlet attacks — represents a fairly straightforward response to Pope's critics. What is not so obvious is that the letters Pope published in 1729, 1735, 1737 and 1741 equally represent a kind of rebuttal.

Pope had learned from Dennis, appropriately enough, that the publication of personal letters might be used in a course of attack and defence. In July 1729 Dennis published a letter Pope had sent him on 3 May 1721 in which Pope requested two sets of Dennis's *Original Letters* and thanked him for the 'Omissions you have been pleas'd to make in those Letters in my Favour'.[10] Dennis included this letter in his *Remarks* on the *Dunciad* to make public what he construed as Pope's hypocrisy in, first, seeming to agree to a cessation of hostilities between them and, then, attacking the critic in that poem.

Pope quickly retaliated in kind. The second edition of the *Dunciad Variorum*, printed in November 1729, included Dennis's letter of 29 April 1721 to which his own had been a reply. In this letter Dennis admitted to removing from *Original Letters* the 'Footsteps' of their previous quarrels. The critic's integrity was thus indicted in the suggestion that, on his receiving Pope's subscription money, Dennis had removed from his publication all passages offensive to Pope.

Lewis Theobald, who had already provoked resentment by his scholarly disparagement of Pope's edition of Shakespeare, offered the poet another opportunity for vindication when he published his own letters. The occasion of their new quarrel was Theobald's publication of a volume of Wycherley's *Posthumous Works* in 1728 which included poetry Wycherley had once entrusted to Pope for revision and which, finally, Pope had advised him against publishing. Knowing that Wycherley had not intended these poems to be made public, that they could not enhance his old friend's reputation and, moreover, that some of the poems contained emendations or insertions supplied by Pope himself, he felt indignation at Theobald over and above the wounds inflicted to his vanity three years earlier by that critic's *Shakespeare Restored*.

In 1729 Pope issued — anonymously, of course — a second volume of Wycherley's Posthumous Works. He included twenty-six letters to and from Wycherley in this volume: eight written by himself and seventeen complete letters and two extracts from letters written by Wycherley. This selection from their correspondence fulfilled three functions. First, Pope's preface 'To the Reader' makes explicit his contempt, dismissing Theobald as one of the greedy adventurers who 'finger'd' Wycherley's inferior, unpublished work after his death 'without any Warrant but their own Arrogance, or motive but their own Lucre'. The accusation is repeated by Pope in his 1735 and 1737 editions in a footnote which deplores the fact that Wycherley's 'Papers . . . having the misfortune to fall into the hands of a Mercenary, were published in 1728'.

Second, Pope publicized the details of Wycherley's request that he 'improve' his poems. Eleven of the twenty-six letters published in 1729 discuss Wycherley's pleas for Pope's assistance, with their correspondence, then, serving as a chronicle of Pope's unsuccessful attempt to transform the mediocre verse, full of repetitions and clumsy phrasing, into passable writing.

Third, this publication of their correspondence illustrated Wycherley's admiration and affection for the young poet. Thirteen of his letters praised Pope, including four commending Pope's witty letters which 'at once pleas'd and instructed', another lauding Pope's 'vigorous Mind', and the two extracts and four other letters extolling Pope's *Pastorals*.

The connection between these Wycherley letters and pamphlet attacks upon himself was drawn by Pope in a footnote to a letter from Wycherley dated 13 May 1708 in which the dramatist told Pope he intended to commemorate his approval of the *Pastorals* by composing a poem in praise of them:

> This, and the following Extract, are a full Confutation of the lying Spirit of **John Dennis** and others, who impudently asserted that Mr. **Pope** wrote these Verses on himself.

The 'Extract' the footnote refers to consists of fragments of Wycherley's letters of 18 May and 28 July 1708 which Pope printed together and which opens with Wycherley's declaration that 'I have made a damn'd Compliment in Verse, upon the printing your Pastorals'. This footnote also appears in the 1735 and 1737 editions.

To ensure a seemingly disinterested publication of these letters to and from Wycherley, Pope had first deposited their correspondence in Lord Oxford's famous Harleian Library. This tactic enabled him, in the preface to his second volume of Wycherley's *Posthumous Works*, to imply that this friend had been solely responsible for their publication; as he explained in a letter to Oxford of October 1729: 'I have made the Publishers say, that Your *Lordship permitted them a Copy* of some of the papers from the Library, where the Originals remain as Testimonies of the Truth'.

In the event, for reasons unknown, the second volume of Wycherley's 'remains' was suppressed.[11] But the failure of this project did not prevent Pope from grasping the wider implications of what he might accomplish by publishing his own letters. Since 1726, when Curll had obtained his letters to Henry Cromwell from his former mistress and published them without permission, Pope had adopted the habit of recalling his own letters, making copies of those he sent, and preserving those which had been sent to him. By September 1729 he was ready to ask Oxford for his consent to deposit not only Wycherley's but also other friends' letters in his library, a request Pope said he had 'had at heart, for half a year &

more'. In this letter to Oxford Pope described his hope that the correspondence he deposited in the Harleian Library might represent a true history of himself and his friends:

> As the rest of the Work I told you of, (that of Collecting the papers & Letters of many other Correspondents) advances now to some bulk; I think more & more of it; as finding what a number of Facts they will settle the truth of, both relating to History, & Criticisme, & part of private Life & Character of the eminent men of my time.[12]

The chronology of events supports a strong link between the pamphlet attacks and Pope's first publication of his general correspondence in 1735. The appearance of the *Dunciad* in 1728 and the *Epistle to Burlington* in 1732 contributed to bring the ephemera warfare relating to Pope to a climax in 1733, which Guerinot describes as a 'year which produced more pamphlets for or against Pope than any other'.[13] It was also in 1733 that Pope, having amassed a large number of letters, initiated his scheme to manoeuvre Curll into publishing them. In that year Pope responded by letter to Curll's advertisement for information for a life of the poet in the anonymous guise of 'P.T.', who offered Curll a 'large Collection of [Pope's] *Letters*, from the former Part of his Days to the Year 1727'.[14]

Pope never admitted responsibility for the 1735 edition of *Letters of Mr. Pope and Several Eminent Persons*, delivered already-printed to Curll and which served as the basis of his *Mr. Pope's Literary Correspondence*, but he did acknowledge the 1737 edition which, as the first volume of the *Works* in prose, was thus presented as the 'genuine, authorized' edition of his correspondence. As Pope's equal involvement in preparing both these editions for the press was conclusively established by Dilke's discovery of the Caryll transcripts in 1864, it is not surprising that the editions are similar. Both editions also bear distinct signs of their relation to the pamphlet attacks.

Both editions begin with a selection of Pope's correspondence with Wycherley. In 1735 Pope added two letters from himself to Wycherley to the eight he had printed in 1729. The first 'new' letter, dated 26 December 1704, opens the section and appears to serve as a formal introduction to Wycherley, identifying him as a friend of Pope's mentor, Dryden, and placing him within the circle of Pope's early friends, Congreve and Trumbull. The second 'new' letter, dated 23 June 1705, echoes one of Pope's favorite complaints: that his friends were too indulgent to him and that they lavished praise on his poetry rather than the criticism it deserved.

Pope somewhat distorted the picture of his epistolary relationship with Wycherley in the 1737 edition by neglecting to show how very two-sided and self-conscious a literary game they played in their early correspondence, heavily indebted as it was to the 'precious' style of letter writing inherited from Balzac and Voiture. This edition substantially reduces Wycherley's contribution, printing only five of his letters, while it includes nine by Pope. Six of Pope's letters object to Wycherley's compliments: a reproof deserved in their correspondence as printed here by Pope, for the letters from Wycherley that he included convey primarily the impression that the dramatist greatly admired the young poet. Too, while Wycherley's letters thank Pope for his friendship and assistance, they do not reply in kind with witty complaints of the flattery contained in Pope's actual letters to him. These distortions are partly attributable to Pope's vanity, but it is also instructive to place them in the context of the many pamphlets which had depicted Pope as a conniving flatterer who had attached himself to the unsuspecting Wycherley.[15]

The selections from his correspondence with William Walsh that Pope printed in 1735 and 1737 equally served to rehabilitate the public image of Pope's relationship with a famous friend. Pamphleteers had, in general, loyally followed the example set by Dennis in his *Remarks* in portraying Walsh's patronage of Pope as a refined form of entertainment or, as Charles Gildon described it in his *Memoirs* of Wycherley, a 'Man of Wit may find an agreeable Diversion in the Company of a pretending Fool sometimes, provided that the Interviews are short and seldome'.[16] The letters Pope printed tell a very different story.

He included six Walsh letters in his 1735 edition and five in the 1737 edition. They serve a variety of functions. If Pope was proud of his friendship with Wycherley, who was widely considered one of his age's greatest writers, he was equally glad of a chance to advertise his intimacy with the eminent critic. Lest his readers failed to grasp Walsh's importance, a footnote in both editions described his as 'Author of several beautiful pieces in Prose and Verse, and in the Opinion of Mr. **Dryden** . . . the Best Critic of our Nation in his time'.

The letters Pope printed reveal that Pope was respected by Walsh as an astute expert on literary matters, with the two friends conversing on terms of equality on such topics as the proper definition of pastoral and pastoral comedy. They show, too, that Pope was not only loved by Walsh as a friend and admired as a critic but that his poetical precocity had early been recognized by him. In the first letter of the Walsh correspondence in the 1735 edition — a letter dropped in 1737 — Walsh recommended the sixteen-year old poet's pastorals to Wycherley in terms of a gratifying comparison: '**Virgil** had written nothing so good at his Age'.

Thus, if we allow that Pope selected for inclusion in his editions those letters to and from Wycherley which might vindicate both his own and the dramatist's reputation (although he cast aspersions on Wycherley's poetical ability in doing so), his selection of Walsh letters for publication followed a similar guideline: they redeemed Walsh from the charge of malice and Pope from that of fawning servility.

The Walsh letters, too, served another purpose. A major topic of this section of correspondence is the sensitive issue of literary 'borrowing'. The charge of plagiarism had dogged Pope for many years; here he could air Walsh's belief that Pope only followed literary tradition in drawing from classical precedent or, as Walsh observed in a letter Pope printed in both editions:

> in all the common Subjects of Poetry, the Thoughts are so obvious (at least if they are natural) that whoever writes last, must write things like what have been said before . . . it being evident in all such Cases, that whoever live first, must first find them out.

Pope also carefully selected and edited letters for publication in 1735 and 1737 which might explain his troubled relationship with a third famous friend — Addison. From 1714 until Pope's death a favorite accusation levelled at him by the pamphlets was that he had viciously turned against his erstwhile patron, the great Addison, who 'rais'd from Dust th' ungrateful Miscreant's Head'. Addison was generally depicted as one of Pope's earliest supporters and, in such pamphlets as *Pope Alexander's Supremacy*, as one of the most active of Pope's friends in procuring subscriptions for the projected *Iliad* translation. This pamphlet, issued in 1729 by Dennis and Duckett, claimed that the fickle Pope, seeing which way the winds of favor blew, had betrayed his old Whig friends and

> listed openly in the **Tory** Service, and every week publish'd scandalous Invectives on those very **Whigs**, who had been his amplest Subscribers.[17]

But, while Pope always maintained that Addison had been the first to encourage him to undertake the translation, Addison apparently did not bother to solicit a single subscriber. He also sponsored and possibly collaborated on Tickell's rival translation and encouraged his circle at Button's coffee house in their manoeuvres to obstruct Pope's success.

It is simplest to consider the Addison letters as printed by Pope in the 1737 edition, where he allotted them a separate section. This section consists of five letters from Pope to Addison, two from Addison to Pope, one from Charles Jervas to Pope and his reply, one to Lord Halifax, four to an unidentified 'Honourable', and one to the 'Hon. James Craggs'. Taken as a whole, these letters present a picture of the rise, growth and betrayal of Pope's affection for Addison. As most of the letters purportedly sent to Addison were demonstrably fabricated from letters Pope originally sent to Caryll, it is most profitable to regard them in the light of a 'story' and to decipher Pope's message in its presentation.

Pope's early letters to Addison are full of expressions of eager admiration, with the 1737 section opening with a letter from him which exclaims: 'I am more joy'd at your return than I should be at that of the Sun'. This is partly, of course, the cant of the Augustan letter-writer's *politesse* exaggerated to the point of humor, but one senses Pope was sincere in his early enthusiasm and respect for Addison. Always a fierce partisan where his friends were concerned, it was this esteem for Addison which prompted Pope's hilarious satire on Dennis, the *Narrative of Dr. Robert Norris*, which is the subject of this first letter and which a footnote in the 1735 and 1737 editions describes as 'occasion'd by **Dennis's** Remarks upon *Cato*'. In the event, Addison was dismayed by Pope's defence of his play and, through Steele, he expressed his disapproval of the pamphlet to its publisher, Lintot. Lintot passed the letter on to Dennis, who printed it in 1729. This unfortunate tale of their early friendship, with Pope's affection rebuffed by Addison, presaged the course of their relationship as chronicled in Pope's editions of their letters.

In the second letter in the 1737 edition, a suspected fabrication, Addison voiced his support for Pope's project: 'I question not but your Translation will enrich our Tongue and do Honour to our Country'. In the context in which Pope prints this letter it represents, as Sherburn has observed, a 'clear indictment of Addison's sincerity.'[18]

The quarrel with Addison presented by Pope in his editions concerns, however, not only the contested *Iliad* translation but also the sensitive issue of party loyalty. Pope's friendship with Swift and Bolingbroke offended Addison's Whig sympathies, who advised Pope in one of his letters to avoid political faction and not to 'content your self with one Half of the Nation for your Admirers, when you might command 'em all' (1735, 199).

In his letters to Addison as well as in the general correspondence he published in 1735 and 1737, Pope portrayed himself as a disinterested spectator of the contemporary political scene who detested the narrowness and animosity bred by the spirit of party so prominent in the early eighteenth century. In one of the letters to Addison Pope drew a parallel between the intolerance and irrationality of party loyalty and the bigotry and dogma of religious fanaticism. Pope could not renounce Catholicism, fearing the pain his apostasy would cause his devout mother, but while religious faith or, at least, the appearance of it, was required, he refused also to adopt any exclusive political allegiances. As he observed in this letter: 'I confess I scorn narrow Souls of all Parties, and if I renounce my Reason in religious Matters, I'll hardly do it in any other' (1735, 200-1). Another letter to Addison concludes: 'I am ambitious of nothing but the good Opinion of good Men, on both Sides' (1735, 207).

The remaining letters in the 1737 edition's section of Addison letters concern, directly or indirectly, Pope's quarrel with him. In his letter of 20 August 1714 to Pope, for example, Jervas recounted his efforts to reconcile the two friends, relating Addison's confession to him that he believed Swift had carried Pope 'too far among the enemy during the heat of the animosity'. Pope's letters to the unidentified 'Hon.' refer more obliquely to Addison in their descriptions of Ambrose Philips' partisan activities; Pope claimed that Philips was not only spreading malicious gossip about his suspected alliance with the Tories but that he also refused to relay to Pope subscription money for the *Iliad* which had been temporarily entrusted to him. The final letter of the section, to Craggs, includes a prose sketch of Addison as an envious 'great Turk in poetry, who can never bear a brother on the throne' which anticipates the 'Atticus' portrait in the *Epistle to Dr. Arbuthnot.*

The 'Atticus' portrait represents another instance of Pope's remarkable facility for learning from his enemies. Just as he learned from Dennis that the publication of a personal letter might serve to answer an attack on him, so he apparently abstracted this famous analogy of the envious Turk from Addison himself. Addison's review of the *Essay on Criticism* in a *Spectator* paper had described a phenomenon he suggested his readers might apply to Pope: 'In our own Country a Man seldom sets up for a Poet, without attacking the Reputation of all his Brothers in the Art'. Addison then proceeded to quote Sir John Denham's verse: 'Nor needs thy juster Title the foul Guild / Of Eastern Kings, who to secure their Reign / Must have their Brothers, Sons, and Kindred Slain'.[19]

In the opportunity for redress offered by a publication of their letters, Pope was anxious to counter not only the charge that he had been ungrateful to Addison but also that he had libelled him posthumously in this portrait, which was first printed in December 1722 in *St. James's Journal*— three years after Addison's death. The 1728 pamphlet *Characters of the Times*, included in the second of Pope's four volumes of attacks, echoed many others in its avowal that its denunciation of Pope was inspired by a need to

> expose the abominable Ingratitude of the Wretch who has dar'd to Insult [Addison] after his Death in a low and stupid Satyr, to insult the Man, to whom

he intirely owes his undeserv'd Success, and to whose too great good Nature he had been so infinitely oblig'd.

Pope acquitted himself of this second charge by adding to the 1737 edition a selection of his correspondence with Francis Atterbury. A letter of 26 February 1722 contained the request that Pope send him a 'compleat copy of those verses on Mr. Addison', with Atterbury adding that the delineation of the satirical portrait was obviously where Pope's 'real strength' lay and suggesting that Pope 'not suffer that talent to lye unemploy'd'. Pope appended a footnote to this letter which absolved him of responsibility for the first publication of the 'Atticus' portrait: 'An imperfect Copy was got out, very much to the Author's surprize, who never would give any'.

Publication of the Atterbury letters afforded another chance to redress the popular pamphlet claim that Pope was a 'rank Papist' and, hence, a treasonable subject plotting the return of the Stuarts to the throne. Atterbury's incarceration in the Tower in 1722, his subsequent conviction of Jacobite treason and exile to France, coupled with the suspicious circumstance of Pope's religion and his close friendship with the former Bishop of Rochester meant, as Pope was fully aware, that these letters would prove of special interest to his contemporaries.

Although Atterbury's guilt was subsequently established, Pope apparently never suspected him. As printed by Pope, their correspondence reveals that the two friends shared a fondness for literary criticism rather than for political conspiracy, and their publication thus gave Pope an opportunity to clear his own name and publicly to air his belief in Atterbury's innocence.

Pope's surreptitious publication of an edition of *Letters Between Dr. Swift, Mr. Pope, &c.* in 1741, which he reprinted in the second volume of his *Works* in prose represented yet another opportunity for him to vindicate his own reputation and that of some of his closest friends. The second volume of Pope's *Works* in prose also included the *Memoirs of Martinus Scriblerus*, and the letters defended, appropriately enough, his relationship with former Scriblerians.

His association with the Scriblerus Club was a popular target of pamphlets attacking Pope. One of 1727 entitled *Gulliver Decypher'd*, for example, was devoted mainly to ironical 'proofs' that Gay, Pope and Arbuthnot had 'maliciously Father'd' *Gulliver's Travels* on Swift, but it deviated from this task to offer caricatures of each of them and to satirize their friendship. Gay's dependency on the patronage of the Duchess of Queensberry was mocked, while the three friends jointly were reviled for combining, in such works as *Three Hours After Marriage*, to form an 'Alliance offensive and defensive between each other'. This pamphlet, included in the second of Pope's four volumes, obviously attracted his attention. His copy is marked by X's and a number of underscorings; Pope also added an explanatory footnote and supplied names of individuals identified only by their initials.

A pamphlet of 1728, *The Twickenham Hotch-Potch*, similarly denigrated Arbuthnot, Swift, Gay and Pope by characterizing them, respectively, as an 'impertinent *Scotch*-Quack, a Profligate *Irish*-Dean, the Lacquey of a Superanuated Dutchess, and a little virulent Papist'.[20] *The Metamorphosis*, also published in 1728, narrowed its attack to Swift and Pope, likening them to dogs, a '*Spaniel P–p–e*, a *Mastiff Sw–t*', that indiscriminately 'teize and bite what'er came next 'em, / But of pure Spite, tho' nothing vext 'em'. Pope's and Swift's literary collaborations were accordingly described as inhuman, malicious ravings: 'To bark, to insult, to run stark wild, / And foam at Woman, Man, and Child; To *foul* and *dirt* each Place they came in, / And play some Pranks, unfit for naming'.[21]

Swift is represented by forty-two letters in *Letters Between Dr. Swift, Mr. Pope, &c.*, Pope by thirty, Bolingbroke by seven, and Gay by three. This collection is augmented by seven 'new' letters in the second volume of Pope's *Works* in prose, including six additional letters written by Swift and a letter from Lord Orrery which deflects from Pope the responsibility for the first publication of correspondence with Swift. Orrery claimed that Swift had delivered a number of letters to an unidentified individual who might be considering their publication.

Although Bolingbroke had not belonged to the Scriblerus Club, Pope's inclusion of his letters in this volume is partly attributable to the fact that he occasionally collaborated with him on letters to Swift. Also, in Swift's absence, Pope had come to rely increasingly on Bolingbroke's support and advice and, in a letter to Swift of 1732, written jointly with Bolingbroke, he suggested that the three friends might form a literary alliance reminiscent of the Scriblerus Club:

> I know nothing that moves strongly but Satire, and those who are asham'd of nothing else, are so of being ridiculous. I fancy if we three were together but for three years, some good might be done even upon this Age; or at least some punishment made effectual, toward the Example of posterity, between History, Philosophy, and Poetry.[22]

That his friendship with Bolingbroke had frequently been condemned in the pamphlets undoubtedly represented one of the reasons Pope included these letters in the 1741 edition. Bolingbroke was usually charged with an attitude of insolence toward his contemporaries, with questionable morals verging on atheism, and with treasonable conduct. In the 1735 *Epistle to Alexander Pope*, for example, Bolingbroke was characterized as Pope's evil genius who unscrupulously misled his friend into supporting his campaign against Walpole's government. Similarly, a 1739 pamphlet entitled *Characters: An Epistle to Alexander Pope Esq.*, written by a 'Walpole hack' to discredit Pope's anti-government satires, accused Bolingbroke of treason and complained that Pope was unduly influenced by him.[23]

The letters Pope published 'answer' these attacks on the Scriblerians in a number of ways. He deleted, for example, references to Gay's dependence on the Duchess of Queensberry's patronage, thus perhaps directly responding to such pamphlets as *Gulliver Decypher'd* and *The Twickenham Hotch-Potch*. Also, he excised from the 1741 edition Swift's criticisms of such mutual friends as Mrs. Howard and the Earl of Burlington, presenting his circle of intimates to the public eye as a united front. There is no talk of politics let alone of treason in this edition but, rather, it is full of the friends' reflections on their aversion to faction, political or religious, and their philosophic indifference to any ambition other than to devote themselves to writing works intended to reform their own and to enlighten future ages. Letter 48 of the second volume of *Works* in prose, for example, is described in the table of contents as

From [Bolingbroke]. Of his studies, particularly a Metaphysical work. Of Retirement and Exercise—Postscript by Mr. P. His wish that their studies were united in some work useful to Manners, and his distaste of all Party-writings.

Pope's presentation of these letters deliberately enhanced the impression that the correspondence constituted the 'story' of a close-knit coterie characterized by its distrust of 'Party-spirit' and by its preoccupation with how one may lead a 'good life'.[24] The pamphlet image of a weak, indolent Gay, a Machiavellian Bolingbroke, and a Swift and Pope who are misanthropic dabblers in dirt and scandal is, thus, carefully undermined by these letters, whose theme might be described as a celebration of friendship and virtue.

The 1741 edition also 'answered' the pamphlets by commemorating the Scriblerus Club and by reaffirming its values; it demonstrated that humanist principles as well as practical reasons underlay their collaborations. The link between the Club and this edition is made explicit by Pope's decision to print the letters and the *Memoirs* together in the second volume of his *Works* in prose. It is made implicitly by the style and content of the letters Pope included, in which Bolingbroke, Swift and

Pope and, occasionally, Gay, join in good-natured mockery of abuses of taste and learning. The rationale behind these letters — and behind Pope's decision to print them — might be traced to Erasmus's letter which prefaces *The Praise of Folly* and dedicates that work to Thomas More: 'How unjust it is to allow every other walk of life its relaxations but none at all to learning, especially when trifling may lead to something more serious!' In publishing their letters, Pope both affirmed and demonstrated the Scriblerian belief in the utility of learned wit.

As for the insidious, because irrational, insinuations throughout the pamphlets which hint that Pope's physical defects were but the visible manifestations of a crippled mind, the letters Pope published in 1729, 1735, 1737, and 1741 represent an answer even to the belief that *mens curva in corpore curvo*. In a letter he sent Caryll shortly after Curll's unauthorized 1726 publication of his letters to Henry Cromwell, Pope accompanied his request that Caryll return his letters with the observation that he believed that his correspondence with 'good men' might vindicate his own character. Cicero's belief, 'friendship cannot exist except among good men', represented a humanist maxim which Pope self-consciously echoes here; as his correspondence

> serve[s] to bear testimony of my own love for good men or theirs for me, I would not but keep [it] on all accounts, and shall think this very article more to my reputation than all my works put together.[25]

The traditional view of Pope's editorship of his own letters holds that his main purpose was to pander to his own ego and that this is confirmed by the fact that Pope readdressed letters originally sent to Caryll to more famous individuals such as Addison and Steele, thereby advertising his intimacy with the great figures of his age. While there is certainly justice in this conjecture, it does not explain the fact that Pope also readdressed some of the Caryll letters to such comparatively obscure friends as Hugh Bethel, Edward Blount and Robert Digby, nor does it account for the fact that he featured his relationship with these three men so prominently in the 1735 and 1737 editions, which include sections devoted to each of them.

Roscoe, in his 1824 edition of Pope's *Works*, offers the most plausible explanation in his observation that 'notwithstanding the acknowledged anxiety of Pope for the establishment of his literary fame', the importance he accorded his friendship with Bethel, Blount and Digby in the *Letters* 'may perhaps incline us to give credit to the asseveration he so frequently makes, that he was still more desirous of being esteemed a good man, than a great poet'.[26]

Of course, one might also see Pope's featuring his intimacy with 'good men' as self-serving. We may return here to Tillotson's point: Pope's reputation after the *Dunciad* was at its shabbiest. Pope's awareness of this is reflected in his collection of pamphlet attacks, which includes a clipping from the *Daily Journal* of 11 May 1728, marked by Pope with lines and X's, which observed:

> this little turbulent Creature has endeavoured to decry and calumniate every Author who has excelled him, and shone in a superior Region to him, moved partly by his natural Envy and Malice, (the Deformity of *Mind* answering to that of his Body) and partly by that Ignorance and Stupidity which makes a Dog howl at the Moon.[27]

Pope also possessed a copy of Giles Jacob's *The Mirrour* which opened with a letter from Jacob to Dennis in which he remarked that, although he had once been content to applaud Pope as 'rising Genius', the publication of the *Dunciad*, with its 'most shameless and unprecedent Abuse of all his Contemporaries, without making any Distinction between Foe and Friend', had provoked Jacob to 'retract [his] good Opinion, and to draw [his] Pen against such an Adversary, and convince him of his great Error, Folly and Madness'.[28]

The letters Pope published serve as a mirror image of that poem. For those who condemned the author of the *Dunciad* as a vitriolic satirist, the letters show Pope in his other capacity: the public poet who denounces vice is revealed in his correspondence as the private individual who loves virtue. While the *Dunciad* dramatically evoked a world of bad writers and faithless friends trembling on the brink of cultural and moral collapse, the 1735, 1737 and 1747 editions of the letters vividly depict a private sphere in which humanist values are restated in contemporary terms. They portray a circle of loving friends dedicated to upholding the banner of civilization bequeathed them by the classical writers. Just as the *Dunciad* had employed Pope's philosophy of the efficacy of a satire based on the example of actual individuals, these three editions operated on the same principle by presenting individuals worthy of imitation.

Pope may have felt that there was a certain ironic justice in 'answering' his detractors with letters in view of the fact that the majority of the pamphlets directed against him and his friends had themselves assumed the form of personal letters. But we must ultimately locate Pope's editorship of his own letters in the philosophy of satire which he explained in a letter to Arbuthnot included in the 1737 edition: 'General propositions are obscure, misty, and uncertain, compar'd with plain, full and home examples'.

The Augustans often ranked biography above history for its value as didactic literature. In his remarks on Plutarch which preface an edition of the *Lives* Dryden commended his work in these terms; it sets 'before us what we ought to shun, or to pursue, by the examples of the most famous men'.[29] In the letters Pope published he not only substantiated his satiric ethos of the good man and the good poet, but he also commemorated his friends by presenting an epistolary tale which taught, by example, what Emrys Jones has identified as the 'great Augustan theme' and a 'lasting pre-occupation of humanism': 'the use of knowledge: how to make knowledge live by making it useful to the real business of learning'.[30]

CONCLUSION

The issue of Pope's publication of his own letters is a broad one subsuming a number of secondary concerns. It is possible to categorize these concerns chronologically, because each age has formulated its own particular protest against Pope's decision to treat his letters as literary artefacts rather than as personal, biographical documents. In Pope's day, the main accusation levelled against Pope was greed: he obviously intended to profit from the editions of his correspondence. On Dilke's discovery of the Caryll transcripts, the Victorians felt that Pope had treated one of his oldest friends shabbily: he had used the actual letters he sent John Caryll as a source for a number of 'invented' or spurious letters to other correspondents. It was assumed that Pope revised his correspondence with Wycherley and Addison, using the letters he had originally sent Caryll, to emphasize his intimacy with these two individuals and to put his own conduct in his relations with them 'in a good light'. Similarly Pope's treatment of Swift has aroused considerable indignation as it has become clear that Pope not only printed his friend's letters in the 1741 edition against considerable opposition but also alleged or, at least, insinuated, that Swift himself had been responsible for this publication.[1] Perhaps Pope's greatest 'crime' for modern scholars is that his editorial practices flouted our notion of the sanctity of the text of original letters.

Pope's desire to profit from the publication of his letters represented a characteristic example of the poet's peculiar genius for making a virtue of necessity; he protected his own interests while accomplishing wider aims. While the letter was recognized as a literary genre in Augustan England, it continued to occupy its old uneasy position as a form of literature whose composition was permissible only when the writer entertained no apparent intention of ultimate publication. Bitter experience had taught Pope that this ambivalent attitude toward the letter simply played into the booksellers' hands. There is no evidence, for example, that he ever benefited financially from Curll's publication of his letters to Cromwell, which were purchased by Curll from his mistress, Mrs. Thomas, for ten guineas and which sold very well.[2]

Pope's elaborate entrapment of Curll, resulting in Curll's 1735 'unauthorized' edition of his letters, highlighted the pressing need for re-

53

form in the publishing trade: laws protected booksellers but not authors. In 1741 Pope sued Curll, who had pirated the quarto edition of Pope's correspondence with Swift in his *Dean Swift's Literary Correspondence*, and in the suit of *Pope versus Curl*, secured the author's copyright in the personal letter.[3] Pope's victory clarified the issue of an author's rights with regard to publications of his letters; the ramifications of this case may be witnessed in the fact that, subsequently, Richardson and Sterne speculated on posthumous publications of their letters in terms of a financial legacy for their descendants.[4]

But the contradiction at the heart of publications of familiar letters persisted. Lord Chancellor Hardwicke, on ruling in Pope's favour in this case, acknowledged the literary value of the letter, but his reluctance to distinguish between letters and 'any other learned work' did not prevent him from assuming an ambiguous stance on letters written deliberately for publication:

> It is certain that no works have done more service to mankind than those which have appeared in this shape upon familiar subjects, and which, perhaps, were never intended to be published; and it is this makes them so valuable; for I must confess, for my own part, that letters which are very elaborately written, and originally intended for the press, are generally the most insignificant, and very little worthy any person's reading.[5]

The irony, of course, is that, in revising his letters, Pope **had** employed 'elaborate' care and **had** intended these letters for the press.

In *Pope versus Curl* Pope not only clarified the ambiguous legal position of letters, affirming their status as literature, but he also aired a pet grievance: that the vulnerable position of an author unprotected by suitable laws meant that either imperfect copies of his works might be pirated by the likes of Curll or spurious pieces attributed to him with impunity. This latter point was an old complaint of Pope's. In the preface to the *Miscellanies* of 1727 Pope bitterly observed that

> the greater Fame a Writer is in Possession of, the more of such Trash he may bear to have tack'd to him. Thus is it apparently the Editor's Interest to insert, what the Author's Judgment had rejected.[6]

Pope's notorious insistence on 'correctness' in his works, a compulsion fostered by Walsh's early advice, gave him a horror of the prospect that work he considered inferior might be stolen or copied and published in his name. He noted in the preface to the 1737 quarto edition of his letters that, unprotected by adequate legislation:

> As an *Author*, you are depriv'd of that Power which above all other constitutes a good one, the power of rejecting, and the right of judging for your self, what

pieces it may be most useful, entertaining, or reputable to publish, at the time and in the manner you think best.[7]

Pope's revision of his letters was consistent with his habit of tireless revisal of his works and with the fact that he never distinguished between his public and private writings. These factors also account for the 1741 edition of Swift's letters. In the early 1730's Swift was alarming Pope by exaggerated reports of mental lapses and illness. Pope's fears for Swift's death — and for his letters — were not alleviated by the letters sent him by Lord Orrery, who relayed stories of troublesome or careless servants in Swift's employ and of Swift's great negligence with his personal papers. Along with his old concern to retrieve as many of his letters as possible, Swift's failing mental powers and Pope's admiration of Swift's epistolary skill constituted a powerful incentive for him to preserve, in the form of suitably edited correspondence, a memorial of their friendship.[8] Orrery's reports of his careless housekeeping, Swift's own accounts of the mediocre company he kept in Dublin, and the alarming frequency with which imperfect copies of Swift's works were stolen and printed without his permission were all circumstances prompting Pope to despair of Swift's intention or even capacity to transmit a worthy image of himself to posterity. Swift's indifference to the fate of his own works was inconsistent with his concern with fame and only explicable with reference to Swift's belief that his writings' significance was so topical that they could not long survive his age.[9]

Pope's anxiety was heightened by his belief that he was to act as Swift's and Bolingbroke's literary executor.[10] Where Swift was too careless, Bolingbroke was too careful. Many of his works were printed at a private press and copies given to a few of his particular friends with the express understanding that these copies were to be considered as manuscripts and not to be circulated.[11] This, of course, was the understanding on which Pope was entrusted with a copy of *The Patriot King*. Considering the fact that Pope kept copies of the letters he and Bolingbroke jointly sent Swift, it is clear that he wanted to publish Bolingbroke's letters as well as Swift's, but simply was unable to procure them.[12] Perhaps, having bequeathed his papers to Bolingbroke, Pope hoped that he might publish their correspondence, but Bolingbroke, furious at the discovery of the 1500 copies of *The Patriot King* Pope had surreptitiously had printed, apparently burned all their letters shortly after Pope's death.

What we may infer from what some have termed Pope's treachery toward both Swift and Bolingbroke is that he was willing to incur Bolingbroke's wrath and even to forfeit his position as Swift's literary executor in his overriding belief in his friends' genius and in his unwillingness that their works be lost to posterity through either carelessness or, in Bolingbroke's case, excessive scrupulousness.[13]

It has been suggested that Pope's prime motive in seeking to publish his letters with Swift 'was pride . . . not simply vanity about his own prose but a touching pride in the fact that he was valued by a man as great as Swift.'[14] This is a serious misreading of facts. While posterity has dealt more kindly with Swift than it has with Pope, the question of their relative fame in the early eighteenth century can be answered by Swift, who observed in a letter of 1737 to Pope: 'My happiness is that . . . the ages to come will celebrate me, and know you were a friend who loved and esteemed me, although I dyed the object of Court and Party-hatred'.[15] In publishing their correspondence in 1741 as well as in collaborating with Swift on the *Miscellanies*, Pope, in fact, accorded Swift the 'high honor of equality with the greatest poet of the age and promised him that honor in perpetuity.'[16] Pope undoubtedly recognized his friend's genius and was proud of vaunting their intimacy, but it was Swift who repeatedly begged the poet to 'immortalize' him in his works.

It is instructive to relate the subterfuges by which Pope published successive editions of his letters to significant precendents in the poet's career. Pope often published works without immediately acknowledging them, a practice dating from the anonymous contributions to the *Spectator* and the *Guardian* up to the *Essay on Man*. His publication of the *Dunciad* might be seen as a rehearsal for his manoeuvres in issuing the 1741 edition, for the original edition of that poem misleadingly described itself as the 'second edition', reprinted in London from the Dublin edition, lending the impression that the work had first been published in Ireland and that Swift was either its author or had collaborated on it.[17]

Pope simply relished intrigue or, as Lady Bolingbroke was fond of observing, Pope 'plaid the politician about cabbages and turnips,' a verdict echoed by Dr. Johnson in his *Life*: he 'hardly drank tea without a stratagem.'[18] A fascinating anecdote recorded by D'Israeli suggests that the oblique paths Pope followed in publishing his own works were entered on at a very early age. According to D'Israeli, Pope was a master of intrigue whose genius 'might have been perhaps sufficient to have organised rebellion':

To keep his name alive before the public, was one of his early plans. When he published his 'Essay on Criticism,' anonymously, the young and impatient poet was mortified with the inertion of public curiosity: he was almost in despair. Twice, perhaps oftener, Pope attacked Pope; and he frequently concealed himself under the name of others, for some particular design.[19]

There was a certain *noblesse oblige* in Pope's habit of using material over and over again in his prose and verse. He apparently believed that his genius prompted and justified disseminating his writings in whatever form was at hand: for example, he abstracted expressions from the private Caryll letters to appear in the public letters to other correspondents. From the considerable body of re-usable literary material represented by the letters he had recalled from Caryll, Pope obviously felt he might plausibly devise letters similar to those he had actually sent to such friends as Wycherley and Addison but which he had failed to preserve in the form of copies.[20]

Pope's failure to include a representative sample of his correspondence with Caryll may be attributable to his reluctance to advertise his intimacy with a fellow Catholic, and particularly one tainted by suspect political leanings, so publicly. Caryll's uncle had fled to France in 1689 to serve as secretary of state for James II, and it is quite possible that this notorious association with the Jacobite cause underlay Pope's unwillingness to visit Caryll at Ladyholt after the early years of their friendship.[21] If Pope was reluctant even to visit Caryll's estate as too conscious a token of their friendship, it is unlikely that he would resign these scruples on editing his letters for publication. Dilke's description of Pope's treatment of an epitaph he had composed on the death of Caryll's uncle affirms Pope's public pose of impartiality and moderation while representing another instance of Pope's amazing ability to re-use his writings:

> as it was the policy of his life never to appear publicly as deeply sympathizing in the concerns of a Pariah caste, he subsequently made other use of this same epitaph — made the first six lines serve to introduce his Whig friend Trumbull; and the remainder was re-cast, and appears as a flourish about Bridgewater in 'The Epistle to Jervas'.[22]

Pope had, in effect, paid a debt of gratitude to Caryll in dedicating *The Rape of the Lock* to him. By the time Pope decided to publish his letters, he was unwilling to accord Caryll that 'idealized patriarchal role in which Pope had portrayed him in earlier and more enthusiastic letters.'[23] Misunderstandings between Caryll and Pope in the 1720's had resulted in estrangement and, for Pope at least, disillusionment. Pope transferred this role to Blount, Digby and Bethel in his editions. The irony in the suggestion that Pope manipulated the text of his letters simply to put himself 'in a good light' is that he suppressed many of his letters to Caryll, including their discussion of charities and acts of kindness on which the friends often collaborated and which occupied so large a part in their actual correspondence.

What particularly struck Pope about the letters Caryll returned was that they constituted an innocent, virtuous story of himself and his friends. He remarked in a letter to Caryll in 1729:

> I have been these 3 weeks in full employment and amusement in reviewing the whole correspondence I have had with 2 or 3 or my most select friends . . . I thank God (above all) for finding so few parts of life that I need be ashamed of, no correspondence or intimacies with any but good, deserving people.[24]

In publishing these letters, Pope was not only indulging purely personal motives but also obeying the Augustan dictum which accorded moral biography the highest importance as a kind of 'teaching by example'. As we have seen, Pope's age preferred its didactic instruction to be delivered in the form of the lives of actual individuals. Richardson's *Pamela* gratified this taste in representing the story of a virtuous individual set within the framework of supposedly genuine personal letters. Pope apparently hoped his own published letters might serve a similar function of 'entertaining and instructing'. A letter from his physician and friend, Dr. Cheyne, to Richardson in 1741 contains the following remark:

> Mr. Pope here charg'd me to make his warm Compliments to you as an honest good Man, and to tell you that he had read Pamela with great Approbation and Pleasure, and wanted a Night's Rest in finishing it, and says it will do more good than a great many of the new Sermons.[25]

Although Pope's *Letters* enjoyed great popularity in the eighteenth century, suspicions of his involvement in their publication as well as changing epistolary and literary tastes contributed to fashion them into a liability in assessments of the poet's posthumous reputation. While *Pamela*, with its delicate exploration of the subjective consciousness, presaged the future of literature and, specifically, of the novel, Pope's letters, rooted in antiquity, based, in particular, on the model of Seneca's moral essays cast into letter form, were doomed to obscurity. Thoroughly grounded in a classical outlook, he insisted always on relating the 'particular' or the contemporary event to timeless, 'general' standards. Pope routinely excised the simply personal or the seemingly trivial from his letters before publication, but even in those unrevised, those published posthumously, there is this same disregard for the minutae of daily existence: news, gossip and scandal. This neoclassical stance ensured Pope's ultimate unpopularity both as letter writer and as poet when changing literary tastes relegated him to the second class of poets because of his failure to write purely from and of himself.[26]

NOTES

NOTES TO INTRODUCTION

1 *The Correspondence of Alexander Pope*, edited by George Sherburn (Oxford: 1956), II, 419.

2 The transcripts, consisting of contemporary copies of the original letters Pope had sent John Caryll, made it clear that Pope had revised his correspondence before publication. See C.W. Dilke's discussion of 'Pope's Writings' in *The Papers of a Critic* (London: 1875), I, 93-342. A detailed discussion of the publication of the letters begins on p. 287.

3 Chapter Five, 'The Self-Portrait in the Letters,' which draws a direct link between the pamphlet attacks on Pope and his decision to publish his letters, appears in *Alexander Pope: Essays for the Tercentenary*, edited by Colin Nicholson (Aberdeen University Press: 1988), 236-252.

NOTES TO CHAPTER ONE

1 For a concise chronology of Pope's actions, see James A. Winn's *A Window in the Bosom* (Hamden, Conneticut: 1977) which includes as an Appendix 'A Timetable of the 1735 Publication,' 203-221.

2 For further bibliographical details of the 1735 and 1737 editions see R.H. Griffith, *Alexander Pope: A Bibliography* (Austin, Texas: 1927), II, 267-374; Vinton Dearing's unpublished Harvard doctoral dissertation, 'A History of the Publication of Alexander Pope's Letters during his Lifetime' (1949); J. McLaverty, 'The first printing and publication of Pope's letters,' The Library, sixth ser., II (1980), 264-280; and *The Prose Works of Alexander Pope*, edited by Rosemary Cowler (Hamden, Conneticut: 1986), II, 319-383.

3 Norman Ault, *New Light on Pope* (London: 1949), 18.

4 George Sherburn prints the *Narrative* in Vol. III, 458-467 of *The Correspondence* and Cowler in *The Prose Works*, II, 327-345. See, too, Sherburn's Introduction, I, xiii.

5 Sherburn, III, 395.

6 *Ibid*, 460.

7 Edmund Curll, *Mr. Pope's Literary Correspondence*, Volume the second, xiii-xiv.

8 *Ibid.*; see also Volume the third, p. iii, in which Curll claims that 'MR. **Pope's** Project to usher his Letters into the World by my Means, was the Foundation of this Scheme of *A Literary Correspondence.*

9 See the anonymous extracts from *Sawney and Colley* (1742) reprinted in *Pope: The Critical Heritage*, edited by John Barnard (London: 1973), 253-262, which include an interesting contemporary footnote to the poem, 260-ln.

10 J.V. Guerinot in *Pamphlet Attacks on Alexander Pope, 1711-1744* (London: 1969) includes, on pp. 309-310, extracts from *The Egotist*.

11 *The Complete Letters of Lady Mary Wortley Montagu*, edited by Robert Halsband (Oxford: 1968), III, 58. As orthography had not yet been regularized, please consider the minor irregularities in spelling, punctuation and capitalization as taken from the original eighteenth-century text as the instances are too numerous to cite individually.

12 Samuel Johnson, *Lives of the English Poets*, edited by George Birkbeck Hill (Oxford: 1905), III, 157.

13 For Broome's and Swift's quotes, see *Correspondence*, III, 512 and IV, 77.

14 *The Works of Alexander Pope, Esq*, edited by Owen Ruffhead (London: 1769), V, 313-14n.

15 *Ibid.*, 313: in Ruffhead's words, Pope's letters 'afford the most perfect model of epistolary writing . . . what principally recommends them, is that frank sincerity, that artless *naïveté* that unaffected openness, which shews the amiable and virtuous disposition of the writer.'

16 *The Correspondence of Thomas Gray*, edited by Paget Toynbee and Leonard Whibley (Oxford: 1935), I, 230.

17 *The Yale Edition of Horace Walpole's Correspondence*, edited by W.S. Lewis (London: 1937-83), Vol. 28, 292.

18 *Lives of the English Poets*, III, 160.

19 *Ibid.*, 208.

20 Sherburn cites this quotation in *The Early Career of Alexander Pope* (Oxford: 1934), 22.

21 In *The Works of Alexander Pope, Esq. in Verse and Prose*, edited by the Rev. William Lisles Bowles (London: 1806), VII, 168, Bowles observes that 'Pope never appears to so much disadvantage, as when he writes to the Ladies.'

22 *The Works of Lord Byron*, edited by Rowland E. Prothero (London: 1901), V, 574; see Appendix III, 522-592 of this volume for the 'Controversy Between Byron and Bowles as to the Poetry and Character of Pope'.

23 The Rev. Alexander Dyce, for example, editor of the 1866 Aldine Edition of *The Poetical Works of Alexander Pope* (London: 1866) in his 'Memoir of Pope' concluded that 'Considering the turbulent and shameless character of Curll evinced in his publications it is not impossible but [he and conspirators may have arranged] this dark and intricate transaction,' I, cx. Adolphus William Ward, editor of the 1869 Globe Edition of *The Poetical Works of Alexander Pope* (reprinted in London: 1956), also had his doubts; see I, xl-xli.

24 Ault, *New Light on Pope*, 14, offers this succinct account of the Caryll transcripts. See also Dilke's *The Papers of a Critic*, I, 93-342.

25 Sherburn, *Early Career*, 20.

26 Elwin-Courthope, Introduction, I, xxvi-xxvii.

27 Sherburn, *Early Career*, 22.

28 Ward, xli, li.

29 Leslie Stephen, *Alexander Pope* (London: 1880), 155.

30 Edith Sitwell, *Alexander Pope* (London: 1930), 16-17.

31 Sherburn, *Early Career*, 20-1.

32 Ault, *New Light on Pope*, 15.

33 Sherburn, Introduction, *Correspondence*, I, ix.

34 Maynard Mack, untitled review of Sherburn's edition, *Philological Quarterly*, 36 (July, 1957), 394.

35 *Ibid.*, 390, 394.

36 John Butt, 'Pope Seen Through His Letters,' *Eighteenth-Century English Literature*, edited by James L. Clifford (New York: 1959), 63.

37 'Pope: The Man and the Poet,' *Of Books and Humankind*, edited by John Butt (London: 1964), 76.

38 Archibald C. Elias's review of James Winn's *A Window in the Bosom* in *The Scriblerian*, 10 (Autumn, 1977), 40.

NOTES TO CHAPTER TWO

1 John Butt, *English Literature in the Mid-Eighteenth Century*, edited and completed by Geoffrey Carnall (Oxford: 1955), 41.

2 William Henry Irving, *The Providence of Wit in the English Letter Writers* (Durham, North Carolina: 1955), 41.

3 Conyers Middleton, *The History of the Life of Marcus Tullius Cicero* (London: 1741), The Preface, xxx.

4 *Ibid.*, xx.

5 *Selected Epistles or Letters out of M. Tullius Cicero*, 'Adapted to the Humour of the Present Age' by Tom Brown (London: 1702), 28.

6 Cicero himself regarded it as a 'pretty composition' and advised Atticus to borrow it from Lucceius; see R.G. Levens, *A Book of Latin Letters* (London: 1930), 80n. In *A Window in the Bosom* Winn argues, on pp. 49-50, that Cicero, like Pope 'had publication in mind even when protesting his negligence,' and the orator observes, 'There is no collection of my letters, but Tiro has about seventy, and some can be got from you. These I ought to see and correct, and then they may be published.' Winn asserts that 'This is a crucial bit of evidence, for it argues that Cicero, like Pope, was not only ready to write in a relatively candid, unrehearsed style, but sensed the worth and interest of what he had written in that way, and was willing to see it published.' A number of

classical scholars concur, however, in believing that Cicero's project of issuing a selection of his correspondence came to nought, and that the nearly one thousand of his letters which have survived have been transmitted to posterity without the orator's care of supervision. See, for example, *Cicero: The Secrets of his Correspondence*, by Jerome Carcopino, (London: 1959), I, 4-14; L.P. Wilkinson, *Letters of Cicero* (London: 1959), 11-14; *Cicero's Letters to Atticus*, edited by D.R. Shackleton Bailey (Cambridge: 1965), I.

7   Winn's *A Window in the Bosom*, 45.

8   *The Letters of Marcus Tullius Cicero to Several of His Friends*, 'With Remarks by William Melmoth' (London: 1753), II, 191.

9   Levens, xvii.

10 It was generally recognized that Seneca invented the essay genre in his *Epistulae Morales*; Francis Bacon's dedication of his own essays to Prince Henry thus observes of the term 'essay' that: 'The word is late, but the thing is auncient. For Senecaes Epistles to Lucilius, yf one marke them well, are but Essaies, that is, dispersed Meditacions, thoughe conveyed in the forme of Epistles,' (Robin Campbell includes this quotation in his edition of Seneca's *Letters from a Stoic* [Harmondsworth: 1969], 21).

11 *The Epistles of Lucius Annaeus Seneca*, edited by Thomas Morell (London: 1786), I, 22, 33.

12 Levens, xvii.

13 *Ibid.*, 152.

14 *The Letters of Pliny The Consul*, 'With Occasional Remarks by William Melmoth' (London: 1747), 332, 342-3.

15 See Wilkinson's edition of *Letters of Cicero*, 14, in which he describes Petrarch's discovery of Cicero's letters as 'one of the most momentous occasions of the Renaissance,' and then goes on to quote from Petrarch's open letter to his hero.

16 Morris Bishop, *Petrarch and His World* (London: 1964), 278.

17 *Ibid.*, 280.

18 Irving recounts this story, 38-9.

19 See Katherine Gee Hornbeak's 'The Complete Letter Writer in English, 1568-1800,' *Smith College Studies in Modern Languages*, XV (1934).

20 Richmond Bond, 'Eighteenth-Century Correspondence: A Survey,' *Studies in Philology*, 33 (1936), 572.

21 See Halsband's introduction to the first volume of *The Complete Letters of Lady Mary Wortley Montagu*, xiv.

22 *Memoirs of Mrs. Laetitia Pilkington* 1712-1750 (New York: reprinted 1928), 60.

23 *Selected Letters of Samuel Richardson*, edited by John Carroll (Oxford: 1964), 317.

24 See *New Letters to the Tatler and Spectator*, edited by Richmond Bond (Austin, Texas: 1959), 10-11 and *The Spectator*, edited by Donald F. Bond (Oxford: 1965), II, 544.

25 *The Works of William Walsh*, included in *The Works of the most celebrated Minor Poets* (London: 1749), II, Preface.

26 Cited in Irving, 108.

27 Jeffrey Hart, *Viscount Bolingbroke: Tory Humanist* (London: 1965), 5.

28 *The Epistles of Lucius Annaeus Seneca*, edited by Thomas Morell, I, 17.

29 Sherburn, *Correspondence*, III, 102-3.

30 *Selected Letters of Samuel Richardson*, 230.

31 *The Tatler*, edited by George A. Aitken (London: 1898-9), IV, 375.

32 C. W. Dilke made this remark in reference to Pope's letters in *The Papers of a Critic* (London, 1875), I, 287.

33 Rosemary Cowler, 'Shadow and Substance: A Discussion of Pope's Correspondence,' *The Familiar Letter in the Eighteenth Century* (Lawrence, Kansas: 1966), 34.

34 Lord Orrery, *Remarks on the Life and Writings of Dr. Jonathan Swift* (London: 1752), 221-2.

NOTES TO CHAPTER THREE

1 Sherburn, *Correspondence*, II, 112.

2 Dr. Johnson, *Lives of the English Poets*, III, 201.

3 *Ibid.*, 201n.

4 *The Works of William Walsh*, II, Preface.

5 Sherburn, *Correspondence*, I, 69.

6 *Ibid.*, III, 92, 101-3, 505.

7 *Letters Upon Several Occasions* (London: 1696), 19.

8 Sherburn, *Correspondence*, I, 111.

9 *Ibid.*, I, 155.

10 *Ibid.*, II, 41.

11 Sherburn, *The Early Career*, 298.

12 *The Tatler*, I, 5; Joseph Spence, *Observations, Anecdotes and Characters of Books and Men*, edited by James M. Osborn (Oxford: 1966), I, 196.

13 Sherburn, *Correspondence*, II, 253.

14 In *The Honest Muse* (Oxford: 1967), Rachel Trickett makes the point on p. 156 that Pope was 'born to books by inclination, but he was born to retirement perforce.'

15 Sherburn, *Correspondence*, I, 353.

16 *Ibid.*, II, 23.

17 *The Prose Works of Alexander Pope*, collected and edited by Norman Ault (Oxford: 1936), I, lvii-lxxii.

18 *The Spectator*, III, 150.

19 See Ault's discussion of these papers, *The Prose Works*, I, lxv-lxvii, lxx-lxxii.

20 *The Guardian*, no. 106, Monday, July 13, 1713, reprinted in *The Prose Works*, I, 130.

21 *The Guardian*, no. 172, Monday, September 28, 1713, reprinted in *The Prose Works*, I, 142-4.

22 Sherburn, *Correspondence*, I, 307.

23 Of course, Pope's poetry of the 1730's was highly political; see Maynard Mack's stimulating discussion of Pope's satiric tactics as he came to make politics a major theme in his later verse in *The Garden and the City* (Toronto: 1969). On the other hand, what Mack identifies elsewhere as Pope's 'desire to impress posterity' with a 'serenity of discourse upon themes of permanent and general significance' led to a marked avoidance of purely political material in his letters, and particularly in those Pope himself edited for publication; see Mack's essay on Pope's letters to Atterbury in the Tower (1945) included in his edition of essays, *Collected in Himself* (London: 1982), 125-33.

24 Sherburn, *Correspondence*, I, 368.

25 *Ibid.*, III, 490.

26 *Ibid.*, I, 160. For Pope's suspected borrowings, see Ault's introduction to *The Prose Works*.

27 *Ibid.*

28 Winn, *A Window in the Bosom*, 18; Ault, *New Light on Pope*, 15.

29 Elwin and Courthope cite this anecdote, I, xxix: 'Curll, in his reply in 1729 to the attack on him in the Dunciad, after noticing Pope's affected depreciation of [the letters to Cromwell], says, "However, they sell very well; price 5s".'

30 Sherburn, *Early Career*, 21; Ault, *New Light on Pope*, 16.

31 Sherburn, *Correspondence*, II, 419.

32 *Ibid.*, see II, 423, 501, III, 79n. 478, 498, 505n, 510.

33 Dearing, 40.

34 See *Correspondence*, III, 38, 101. Pope sent his letter of 9 April 1730 jointly with Bolingbroke in response to Swift's letter accusing him of 'Schemes of Epistolary Fame': this letter could scarcely have reassured Swift, and it is interesting that, in publishing this letter in 1741, Pope deleted his own portion of it, thus excising not only his disclaimers to such 'Schemes' but also this indication that he had begun to assemble a volume of Swift's letters as early as 1730.

35 See Sherburn's *Correspondence*, I, 479-83, 494-500. Dearing conjectures that the 'general coincidence of expression' characterizing these letters suggests that Pope and Gay jointly composed a draft and that 'free variations were sent by either or both to their friends'; see Dearing, 255-6.

36 See Sherburn's *Correspondence*, II, 278n. In his review of Sherburn's Correspondence (1957), Maynard Mack noted Pope's predilection for repeating this 'analogy of his mother's precarious life to the risings and fallings of a

dying taper' and remarked upon the emergence of this image, in significantly altered form, in the *Epistle to Cobham*; see *Collected in Himself* 157-8.

37 Ault, *The Prose Works*, I, xlv.

38 *The Spectator*, III, 41.

39 John Donne, *Letters to Severall Pesons of Honour* (1651), a facsimile reprint with an introduction by M. Thomas Hester (New York: 1977), 105-6.

NOTES TO CHAPTER FOUR

1 Geoffrey Tillotson, *Pope and Human Nature* (Oxford: 1958), 153.

2 *Lives of the English Poets*, III, 188.

3 Guerinot, xxviii.

4 These four volumes are preserved in the British Library, pressmark C.116.b.1-4.

5 See John Dennis's *Remarks* (London: 1711), 26-30 for the above quotations. In Pope's copy of this pamphlet, included in the first of the four volumes, he inked Wycherley's name in Dennis's assertion that the poem praising the *Pastorals* had misleadingly been 'published in Mr. W.—'s Name'. He also underlined 'ancient Wit' and identified him as Wycherley in the margin.

6 John Dennis, *A True Character of Mr. Pope And His Writings* (London: 1716), 10. In Pope's copy of this pamphlet, included in the first volume, he marked these comments with a line down the margin and with two X's.

7 Lady Mary Wortley Montagu, *To the Imitator Of The Satire Of The Second Book of Horace* (London: 1733), 7.

8 See Guerinot, xxxi, and Bonamy Dobrée, *Alexander Pope* (London: 1951), 51.

9 Sherburn, *Correspondence*, I, 132; II, 343-4, 481.

10 See Dennis's *Remarks Upon Several Passages in the Preliminaries to the Dunciad* (London: 1729), 40.

11 A number of reasons have been offered: Curll believed that Pope had himself bought up all the copies to re-use the sheets in the first edition of his general correspondence in 1735; it is possible that Lintot objected to the edition as an infringement on his copyright on two poems reprinted in it; or it may simply have transpired that Pope was unable to find a sufficient number of purchasers. For these theories, see Elwin and Courthope's edition of Pope's *Works*, V, 283; *Ault's New Light on Pope*, 17; and Vinton Dearing's 'Pope, Theobald, and Wycherley's *Posthumous Works*', PMLA, LXVIII (1953), 236.

12 Sherburn, *Correspondence*, III, 54.

13 Guerinot, xxiv.

14 Sherburn, *Correspondence*, III, 395.

15 For this type of accusation, see *Characters of the Times* (London: 1728) which describes Pope as a 'little flatterer of, and Hanger upon the late Mr. Wycherley'. This pamphlet is included in the second of Pope's four volumes.

16 Charles Gildon, *Memoirs Of the Life Of William Wycherley* (London: 1718).

17 *See Mr. P[O]PE's Picture in Miniature* (London: 1743), 5. *Characters of the Times* similarly had asserted that "When [Pope] first set up for an Author, his Works lay for some Years the Refuse and Rubbish of the Booksellers Stalls, and had continued in the same obscurity until this Day, had not Mr. **Addison**, out of his uncommon Generosity, taken Notice of him . . . No sooner had our great **Addison** given him a Figure in the Eye of Mankind, but he set himself to abuse and ridicule him, and all his Acquaintance'.

18 Sherburn, *Correspondence*, I, 196n.

19 *The Spectator*, II, 482.

20 See *The Twickenham Hotch-Potch* by Caleb D'Anvers (London: 1728), vi.

21 See *The Metamorphosis* by Jonathan Smedley (London: 1728), 5.

22 Sherburn, *Correspondence*, III, 276.

23 See Guerinot, 276-7. In *Characters* (London: 1739) Pope was advised: 'Now drop with **St. John** to the deepest Hell, / And unto Traitors there your Poems sell: / There let your hawkers cry 'em on a String, / And spread Sedition to dethrone your King. / Yet blot out all Encomiums ere you vend, / With which you dawb and flatter ev'ry Friend; / Or you'll be scourged severely for a Fool, / And double damn'd for an **Apostate's** Tool'.

24 For an extensive catalogue of Pope's revisions, see Dearing's thesis, op. cit., and Archibald C. Elias's unpublished Yale Ph.D. (1973) on 'Johathan Swift and Letter Writing'.

25 Sherburn, *Correspondence*, II, 419.

26 Roscoe's edition of Pope's *Works* (1824), VIII, 344; IX, 255.

27 This excerpt is included in Pope's second volume in *A Compleat Collection* (London: 1728) — consisting of all the verses, essays, letters and advertisements on the *Dunciad.*

28 See the third of Pope's four volumes; *The Mirrour* consisted of twenty letters, followed by an 'Addenda' chronicling the 'legal **Tryal** *and Conviction of Mr.* **Alexander Pope** of Dulness and Scandal'. Pope was found 'guilty' of these charges in his 'nonsensical and filthy *Dunciad*; his sentence: 'the said **Alexander** was the same Day cast down from the high Mount of **Parnassus**, no longer to be rank'd among the Poets of Fame'.

29 See Dryden's *Life of Plutarch* prefixed to *Plutarch's Lives* (Edinburgh: 1757-8), I, 1.

30 Emrys Jones, *Pope and Dulness*, Chatterton Lecture (London: 1968), 250. In 'The Muse of Satire' (1950) Maynard Mack distinguishes three Popean personas prominent in his satiric poems; the ethos Pope establishes in his letters is that of the first 'voice' Mack describes, that of the **vir bonus,** the 'man of plain living, high thinking, lasting friendships; who hates lies, slanders, lampoons; who laughs at flatteries of himself; who is "soft by Nature, more a Dupe than Wit"; who loves of all things best "the Language of the Heart"'. See

Collected in Himself, 55-64. As for the motives underlying Pope's publication of his own letters, Mack succinctly outlines the major ones in his *Life* of the poet: 'It was part of his effort to set the record straight, garner up the fruits of his career, project an edifying image to the after time, communicate his deep belief in the social worth of the poetic function, and erect a monument to himself and the gifted group of writers he had known'; see *Alexander Pope: A Life* (London: 1985), 660-662.

NOTES TO CONCLUSION

1 Irvin Ehrenpreis includes a detailed account of the complicated intrigues accompanying the first publication of Swift's and Pope's letters in the third volume of his biography of *Swift: The Man, His Works, and the Age* (Cambridge, Massachusetts: 1962-83), 883-898. See also Mack's *Life*, 665-671.

2 See Frank Arthur Mumby's *Publishing and Bookselling* (London: 1930), 194.

3 See J. McLaverty's persuasive argument in 'The first printing and publication of Pope's letters,' 264-80; Henry Ransom, 'The personal letter as literary property,' *Studies in English*, 30 (1951), 116-31; and Pat Rogers, 'The Case of Pope v. Curll,' *The Library*, 5th ser. XXVIII (1972), 326-31.

4 See John Carroll's introduction to *Selected Letters of Samuel Richardson* and Lewis Perry Curtis's introduction to *Letters of Laurence Sterne* (Oxford: 1935).

5 See excerpts from the summation of the case included in George Harris's *The Life of Lord Chancellor Hardwicke* (London: 1847), I, 540.

6 *Miscellanies in Prose and Verse* (London: 1727-35), I, Preface, 11.

7 Sherburn reprints this preface in *Correspondence*, I, xxxvi-xl, and Cowler in *The Prose Works*, II, 368-72.

8 In a letter Pope sent Swift in August 1736 he asserted that 'You are a very ignorant man; you don't know the figure [Bolingbroke's] name and yours will make hereafter: I do, and will preserve all the memorials I can, that I was of your intimacy;' see Sherburn's *Correspondence*, IV, 28.

9 Swift, for example, evinced a scrupulous concern for Gay's posthumous reputation that he never exhibited toward his own: see Sherburn's Correspondence III, 361 and V, 12. In a letter to Pope of 1723 Swift admitted envying Pope the political neutrality of his profession: 'Your happiness is greater than your Merit in chusing your Favorites so Indifferently among either party, this you owe partly to your Education and partly to your Genius, employing you in an Art where Faction has nothing to do. For I suppose Virgil and Horace are equally read by Whigs and Toryes'; see *Correspondence*, II, 199. As for Swift's carelessness with his own papers, see, for example, the prefatory letter addressed to Pope by the anonymous individual who published the first version of Swift's poem on himself as *The Life and Genuine Character of Doctor Swift* (London: 1733). This mysterious 'L.M.' remarked that he had obtained a copy of the work easily, without Swift's knowledge or consent.

10 In a letter he sent Pope on 12 June 1732 Swift observed: 'I have order'd by my Will, that all my Papers of any kind shall be deliver'd you to dispose of as you please;' see *Correspondence*, III, 291. As for Pope's belief that he was to serve as Bolingbroke's literary executor as well, see William Warburton's 'A Letter to the Editor of the Letters,' included as Appendix II in *The Life of Alexander Pope* by Owen Ruffhead in the fifth volume of Ruffhead's edition of Pope's *Works*, 451.

11 See George Wingrove Cooke's *Memoirs of Lord Bolingbroke* (London: 1785), II, 214.

12 H.T. Dickinson, author of *Bolingbroke* (London: 1970), observed in the course of a conversation with me that the scarcity of letters surviving between Pope and Bolingbroke might be attributable to Bolingbroke's probable request that Pope destroy the letters he sent him, lest they ultimately fall into the government's hands. See also *Correspondence*, IV, 271n, where Sherburn remarks that 'Pope may have preserved much of his correspondence with Bolingbroke, but his will left all MSS. to Bolingbroke, and as a result we have almost no letters for this period [early 1740's] to or from his lordship.'

13 Incurring Swift's displeasure over the publication of their letters may have been a prime reason why Pope lost Swift's bequest. In 1740 Swift wrote a new will which left Pope only a miniature painting of the first Lord Oxford; see Herbert Davis, *The Prose Works of Jonathan Swift* (Oxford: 1939-68), XIII, 154. Elias believed, too, that this issue was one of the main reasons why Swift withdrew his bequest, although he also pointed out that Swift may simply have conceived doubts over making Pope his literary executor in view of Pope's treatment of his *History of the Four last Years of the Queen, Verses on the Death of Dr. Swift* and the *Libel on Dr. Delany* as, on being entrusted them by Swift for inspection, Pope, with his obsession with revision, had excised parts of the latter two works preparatory to their publication and rewritten parts of all three; see Elias 169-71 and 201-4.

14 Winn, *A Window in the Bosom*, 195-6.

15 Sherburn, *Correspondence*, IV, 72.

16 Austin Warren, *Alexander Pope as Critic and Humanist* (Princeton: 1929), 261.

17 See Thomas R. Lounsbury, *The First Editors of Shakespeare* (London: 1906), 230.

18 Dr. Johnson, *Lives of the English Poets*, III, 200.

19 Isaac D'Israeli, *Miscellanies of Literature* (1796, republished London: 1840), 186, 180-1.

20 Sherburn has observed that his 'public would have considerable interest' in letters to these individuals and would wonder why none appeared in Pope's editions; see *Early Career*, 21. Ault believed that, from the considerable body of re-usable literary material represented by the letters he had recalled from Caryll, Pope obviously felt he might plausibly devise letters similar to those he had actually sent these friends but which he had failed to preserve in the form of copies; see *New Light on Pope*, 16. Finally, Dearing, who has made an exten-

sive bibliographical study of Pope's letters, including the surviving originals, contemporary transcripts, and has analyzed the revisions made by Pope in his various editions, has concluded that 'we cannot prove that Pope had any reason to believe that phrases written to his old and intimate friend, Caryll, were misleading in letters to Addison'; see Dearing's thesis, 159.

21 Howard Erskine-Hill, *The Social Milieu of Alexander Pope* (London: 1975), 97.

22 Dilke, *Papers of a Critic*, I, 126.

23 Erskine-Hill, 77.

24 Sherburn, *Correspondence*, III, 38.

25 Manuscript LA III. 356, Special Collections Department, University of Edinburgh Library, 92.

26 As early as 1756 Joseph Warton in *An Essay on the Genius and Writings of Pope* had initiated the process of attrition which would wear down Pope's reputation throughout the next century and a half in drawing his famous distinction between a 'MAN OF WIT, a MAN OF SENSE, and a TRUE POET,' which served to relegate Pope to the second class of poets; see Warton, *An Essay*, 2nd ed. (London: 1762), I, iv. Warton's Romantic sensibility logically damned Pope's letters as well as his poetry. In his 1797 edition of Pope's *Works* Warton accorded the letters of some of Pope's correspondents — Swift, Arbuthnot, Peterborough and Trumbull in particular — special praise as 'written from the heart, and in an easy, familiar style.' Those by Bolingbroke, however, Warton described as 'in the form of dissertations', and he compared Pope's to the 'elegant and studied Epistles of Pliny and Balsac . . . They seem to be chiefly valuable for some literary particulars incidentally mentioned'; see *The Works of Alexander Pope*, edited by Joseph Warton (London: 1797), I, lix.

Made in the USA
Monee, IL
07 July 2026

56551543R00039